FEAR NOT

G000138740

Compiled by

B. McCALL BARBOUR

Published by
B. McCALL BARBOUR
28 George IV Bridge, Edinburgh EH1 1ES, Scotland

First Edition

(in this form)

1976

Reprinted 1984

© B. McCall Barbour

ISBN 0 7132 0025 1

Made and Printed in Great Britain by
Stanley L. Hunt (Printers) Ltd, Midland Road, Rushden, Northants

FEAR NOT!

Freedom from fear is God's Will

"I will trust, and not be afraid."—Isa. xii. 2.

"FREEDOM from fear, at all times and under all circumstances, is the will of God for His people. The trust and love which He desires, and imparts, casts out the fear that springs from unbelief. . . . Fearlessness, we affirm, is the prerogative of the child of God, and, in so far as a man is possessed by Christ, will he be liberated from fear. Where He is, fear takes flight, as darkness vanishes before the light. 'It is I, be not afraid.' His resurrection greeting and gift was peace; 'Peace from Him which is, and which was, and which is to come.' The hearts that enthrone Omnipotence, dwell in the secret place of the Most High, and abide under the shadow of the Almighty, and may well exclaim: 'Therefore will not we fear, though the earth be removed and the mountains be carried into the midst of the sea'. Far beneath the restless, swelling billows there is peace:

'Peace, perfect peace, with sorrows surging round?
On Jesus' bosom nought but calm is found.'

The Roman Emperor threatened Chrysostom with banishment if he still remained a Christian. He replied: 'Thou canst not, for the world is my Father's house; thou canst not banish me.' 'But I will slay thee,' said the Emperor. 'Nay, but thou canst not,' said the noble champion of the faith, 'for my life is hid with Christ in God.' 'I will take away thy treasures.' 'Nay, that thou canst not,' was the retort, 'for, in the first place, I have none that thou knowest of; my treasure is in heaven, and my heart is there.' 'But I will drive thee away from man, and thou shalt have no friend left.' 'Nay, that thou canst not,' once more said the faithful witness, 'for I have a Friend in Heaven from Whom thou canst not separate me. I defy thee; there is nothing thou canst do to hurt me!'

'Fear Him, ye saints, and you will then
Have nothing else to fear.' "

—Ida D. Martin.

"The soul that on Jesus hath leaned for repose,
I will not, I will not desert to its foes:
That soul, though all hell should endeavour to shake,
I'll never, no never, no never forsake!"

PEACE—WHAT IT IS

"The Lord of peace Himself give you peace always by all means. The Lord be with you all."—II Thess. iii. 16.

"PEACE is promised to those whose hearts are stayed on God. 'Thou wilt keep him in perfect peace whose mind is stayed on Thee.' What, then, is the nature of this possession so wonderfully bestowed and preserved to us by God Himself? Peace is that settled calm happiness which is more quiet and lasting than joy,—more noble and worthy than pleasure. Pleasure may make us for a time forget pain, and a passing joy may take for a moment the place of a passing sorrow, but peace is deeper than these. Search the heart in which true peace dwells, and you will find it reaching down to the centre of life itself; pleasure, pain, joy, sorrow, may come and go, but peace abides through all.

It is remarkable that in the books and in the talk of the men of this world you rarely find the word 'peace.' They seem to have found the thing itself beyond their reach; the life of peace appears to them an impossible condition here. You sometimes hear them speak of a tranquil life, but that only means a freedom from external disturbances. Now, the peaceful life of a faithful Christian is not one always of outward quietness. It may be one of constant, busy employment; we have each of us our work to do, and much of this work may be fatiguing, troublesome, full of interruptions, distasteful in itself; and so we may lead anything but what the world means by a tranquil life, and yet it may be full of peace.

> 'There are in this loud stunning tide
>   Of human care and crime,
> With whom the melodies abide
>   Of th' everlasting chime;
> Who carry music in their heart
>   Through dusky lane and wrangling mart,
> Plying their daily task with busier feet,
>   Because their inner souls a holy strain repeat.'

When our Lord said, 'Peace I leave with you, My peace I give unto you,' He added, 'Not as the world giveth, give I unto you.' And, indeed, the peace of His bestowing is as mysterious as the Giver."—*Rev. T. V. Fosbery, M.A.*

FEAR NOT!

HE is ruling all

"Be of good cheer: it is I; be not afraid!"—Mark vi. 50.

"THE comfort of the Lord's people lies in the person and character of Jesus. Here is their solace—'It is I. . . .' But what a big 'I' it is. Compound in one all that is conceivable of goodness, and mercy, and grace, and faithfulness, and love, and perfect humanity, and infinite Godhead, and all the sovereign rights, powers, and possessions of the Highest, and these are all contained in the one little letter 'I' when Jesus says, 'It is I, be not afraid'. . . . The disciples were 'toiling in rowing, for the wind was contrary unto them'. . . . He came up into the ship, and as He stood amid them, the stillness all around proved that the 'I Am' was there. . . . Where the great 'I Am' is present, the winds and the seas perceive their Ruler, and obey. . . . Sin may abound yet more; the light of the Gospel may burn low; and the prince of darkness may widely sway his destroying sceptre; but nevertheless, this standeth sure, that Jesus is the 'I Am'. . . . Look through the darkness, and you shall see your Lord, amid the hurricane, walking on the waters of politics, ruling national convulsions, governing, overruling, arranging all, making even the wrath of man to praise Him, and restraining it according to His wisdom. Above the howling of the blast I hear His Voice announcing 'It is I'. When men's hearts sink for fear, and the rowers feel their oars ready to snap by the strain of useless toil, I hear that word which is the soul of music. 'It is I, be not afraid' —'I am ruling all things. I am coming to the rescue of the barque—My Church: she shall yet float on smooth waters, and reach her desired haven.'"

—*Rev. C. H. Spurgeon.*

"The night wore on, and fiercer grew the conflict,
Higher the waves, more boisterous the wind;
And in the boat, a horror of great darkness
Raised upon each weary heart and mind.
Worse than the storm, more fearful than the tempest
Lay the dark doubt that He Who let them go,
Must have forsaken them, else why this silence?
Did He not *care*—for surely He must know.

Comes the fourth watch, and lo, upon the waters,
In the grey dawn, there move's a distant form!
'Who can *this* be?' they cry in sore amazement—
Is it a ghost, more awful than the storm?
Listen! He speaks! Above the tempest's raging
His voice rings out, so welcome to their ears—
'Be not afraid, for it is, your Master'—
Oh, how it drives away all doubts and fears."

(Ivy M. Fordham.)

PEACE—OUR BIRTHRIGHT

" These things have I spoken unto you, that in Me ye might have peace.   In the world ye shall have tribulation : but be of good cheer ; I have overcome the world."—John xvi. 33.

" PEACE was made in the blood of the Cross. ' Being justified by faith we have peace with God through our Lord Jesus Christ ! ' But there is another peace a believer may have, in the midst of a world of unrest, uncertainty, and constant strain. It is our birthright as children of God to possess the peace of God, rest, calmness, quietness. The Lord Jesus Christ in His life on earth had this peace, and He has left it to us. ' My peace I give unto you ' (John xiv. 27). But the enjoyment of this peace depends on our obedience to His Word, our close fellowship with Himself. ' Thou wilt keep him in perfect peace, whose mind is stayed on Thee : because he trusteth in Thee ' (Isa. xxvi. 3). ' O that thou hadst hearkened to My commandments ! then had thy peace been as a river, and thy righteousness as the waves of the sea ' (Isa. xlviii. 18).

We can have and enjoy great peace. When things go amiss, and we lose the earthly goods and take it all from His hands, knowing He does all things well, we have that peace. When men, often professing Christians, slander, bring wrong accusations, malign and back-bite, it is perfect peace to bring it all into His presence, leave it there, forgive and forget. It is perfect peace when, in all kinds of adversities, we look to Him and praise Him, even for trials and afflictions. And how we need this peace ! Reader, you feel you need it ! You want it ! and it will be yours in walking with the Lord, obedient to His Word, trusting in Him."—*Dr. A. C. Gaebelein.*

FEAR NOT!
True faith accepts God's Will

"I say unto you my friends, Be not afraid of them that kill the body, and after that have no more that they can do."—Luke xii. 4.

"Our God, Whom we serve, is able to deliver us."—Dan. iii. 17.

"TRUE faith accepts the will of God. It does not demand deliverance, but believes that God can deliver; as to whether He will or not, it leaves with Him. God does not always deliver His saints from the hands of tyrants. John the Baptist was allowed of the Lord to die at the will of Herod, as also was James (Acts xii. 2). Those, of whom the world was not worthy, were sawn asunder, slain with the sword, wandered in sheep skins and goat skins, being destitute, afflicted, tormented (Heb. xi. 37). Faith is willing to die for Christ or to live for Him: the decision as to which it shall be is gladly recognized to be the Lord's. So it was with these three Hebrew men. 'Our God, Whom we serve, is able to deliver us,' of that they allowed no question; 'And He will deliver us', was their conviction. But, as it was not based on any promise, they could not assert that He would. If He did not, then they would die; but anyhow, 'Be it known unto thee, O king, that we will not serve thy gods, nor worship the golden image which thou hast set up'. We should thank God for this grand illustration of courageous faithfulness. There are less dramatic and spectacular battles of equal intensity being fought by many an unknown and lowly warrior. 'Courage, brother, do not stumble!' Read this passage, and stand for God. What a contrast we have here! Calm conviction and courage facing rage and fury. 'We are not careful to answer thee in this matter.' The king could hardly believe his ears. All he could do was to order fuel for the furnace, in order to give expression to his own fury; as if a little more or less heat mattered to the young men!. . . . The king was really impotent. 'Be not afraid of them that kill the body, and after that have no more that they can do.' He could have his cruel revenge; but after that—no more."

—*George Goodman.*

"When through fiery trials
Thy pathway shall lie,
My grace all-sufficient
Shall be thy supply;
The flame shall not hurt thee
I only design
Thy dross to consume
And thy gold to refine."

PEACE—TWO KINDS

" Come unto Me, all ye that labour and are heavy laden, and I will give you rest. Take My yoke upon you, and learn of Me ; for I am meek and lowly in heart : and ye shall find rest unto your souls. For My yoke is easy, and My burden is light."—Matt. xi. 28-30.

" TWO kinds of rest are needed by us all :—and they are both in the great uplifting promise of Christ. The one is rest of conscience ; and that rest He says ' *I will give.*' It comes at once. It is not to be laboured for, but to be accepted as a gift of grace. The other is the rest of heart, and that rest He says ' *you shall find* ' : it comes into us gradually, but comes more and more ; the meeker and lowlier, like Him, we become. This was His message to the weary souls that were crushed by the vain strivings and disappointments of life ; restless just because they were putting their own will in the place of God's. . . . Now, what exactly did Jesus mean ? His meaning would be, ' put yourselves into the same relation to God as I am continually in ; cease utterly from your foolish ambitions to be rich, or honoured, or worldly prosperous, or great ; cease, too, from all complainings about your earthly lot, all envyings of other men, all bitter feelings against them or against God ; live, as I am doing, in unquestioning submission to my Father's will concerning Me ; I am meek and lowly in heart, accepting, willingly, the yoke of poverty and homelessness, the burden of humiliation and contempt ; but I find that yoke easy, and that burden light, because I thoroughly acquiesce in my Father's will. Do you the same, and you, too, will find the rest, in which I am living, every day.'

Christ's message, therefore, to the millions of earth's weary souls, is that their cry for rest is often a wholly misdirected cry : for what we need is not that our surroundings should be changed, but that we should be changed ourselves. It is not change of circumstances, nor change of place that will give us rest, but change of heart-feeling and heart-aim : not the world changed to us, but ourselves changed to it. Let that change of feeling come,—our centre will be changed ; and then *will* come to us rest, though all our world should go."

—*Rev. G. H. Knight.*

FEAR NOT!

The stayed and stilled mind

"Sit still . . . until thou know."—Ruth iii. 18.
"Their strength is to sit still."—Isa. xxx. 7.

"OUTSIDE stillness may favour inside calm, but the universal human heart knows well how common the experience is of 'sitting', without being able to 'sit *still*'.

But, is it possible to 'sit still', in a world of such ceaseless activity, and faced, as we so perpetually are, by problems that perplex, and mysteries that amaze? Yes, it is quite possible! This is what Christ can do for those who are His own. 'With God all things are possible' (Matt. xix. 26). Here is the divine recipe for stillness in the midst of doubt, darkness, disturbance and disaster—'*Thou wilt keep him in perfect peace, whose mind is stayed on Thee; because he trusteth in Thee*' (Isa. xxvi. 3). It adds immensely to the meaning of this verse, if we read it in its free translation: 'Thou wilt keep him in perfect peace whose mind *stops at God*'. In other words, the mind that reckons on God in everything, and refuses to go beyond Him; the heart that is satisfied to lean hard on Him, and to leave all its affairs to His almighty wisdom, love and care; the soul that is stayed upon God; such are kept 'in perfect peace', and may blessedly 'sit still'. Here, then, is an ever-open, never-failing harbour of refuge for the sinking spirit, for the exhausted frame, for the troubled mind, for the fearful and foreboding soul. Here is 'a shelter in the time of storm'.

'Stayed upon Jehovah, hearts are fully blest:
Finding, as He promised, perfect peace and rest.'

THERE! O soul, hast thou got 'there'? For, it is only 'there' that we find this stillness that soothes and strengthens, that subdues and sweetens and sustains. Art thou so right with God that thou canst 'stay' upon Him; that thou canst 'stop at God'; unloading every care, and leaving all in His all-loving hands? It is only 'there' that we can 'sit still'. When, through the blood-stained way of Calvary, we have learned something of that love that sought us, bought us, and brought us to His fold, and made us His for evermore, then, surely, we may trust His power to keep us in safety in all our future course, even though it be to us a hidden and mysterious way."

—*B. McCall Barbour.*

"The very dimness of my sight makes me secure
For, groping in my misty way,
I feel His hand, I hear Him say—
'My help is sure'."

PEACE—AS JOINT-HEIRS

" **Therefore being justified by faith, we have peace with God through our Lord Jesus Christ.**"—Rom. v. 1 A.V.

" **Being therefore justified by faith, *let us have* peace with God through our Lord Jesus Christ.**"—Rom. v. 1 R.V.

" WE are brought out of a condition of alienation and separation into one of acceptance and peace. The controversy is ended. There is no condemnation. We are regarded and treated as friends, and received into His family as children and joint heirs with Christ. Now, why should it be said, '*Let* us have peace,' when we have it already ?

There is, doubtless, a very profound reason for it, and perhaps it will appear if we put the emphasis on the word *have*. Let us *have* peace. God has made it, now let us *take* it. Many persons are trying to make peace, but peace is already made through Jesus Christ, and all God asks of us is to *take* the reconciliation that He offers, and *have* the peace that He has arranged. Many persons are acting toward God as if He were at war with them, as if everything were against them, and God was their worst enemy. The truth is, God was in Christ Jesus reconciling the world unto Himself, and the death of Jesus was the outflow of His own personal and sovereign love ; and when we see this, and know it, we are ready to lay down our arms and become His friends. ' Therefore let us have peace.' "

—*Rev. A. B. Simpson, D.D.*

" I need not make my peace with God,
  My Saviour has done that for me ;
For He made peace by His own blood,
  Upon the Cross of Calvary.

By faith I *take* God's gracious peace,
  Because in Christ I'm reconciled ;
My fear and restlessness now cease
  In Christ, Whom peaceless man reviled.

Sweet peace of conscience and of mind
  Is always mine as I obey ;
Because in Christ, my Lord, I find
  The peace of God for every day.

The past need never haunt me more ;
  The present need not have a care ;
For all my sins my Saviour bore,
  And He will all my burdens bear."

(Anon.)

JUNE
14
SUNDAY

The Father, the Word,
and the Holy Ghost:
and these three are one.
1 John 5:7.

I bind unto myself today
The strong Name of the
Trinity;
By invocation of the same,
The Three in One, and One
in Three,
Of whom all nature hath
creation,
Eternal Father, Spirit, Word.

St. Patrick,
tr. Cecil Frances Alexander.

fear is not from God!

FEAR NOT!

We have a Heavenly Father

"Your Heavenly Father knoweth that ye have need of all these things."—Matt. vi. 32.

"HE who frets has lost his God—is indeed, as if God were not. Surely it is worse than having no God to kneel down and say, 'Our Father, Who art in heaven', and then to go forth fretting and fearing, as if He never knew or cared. It is worse than being an orphan, to have a Father and yet forget His love. How perplexed the angels must be at the sight of the fretting child of a Heavenly Father! 'Has he not a Father?' asks one in amazement. 'Does not his Father love him?' says another. 'Does not his Father know all about him?' says a third. 'Is not his Father rich and great?' asks a fourth. 'Has not his Father given us charge concerning him?' say they all; 'how then can he fret?' If there be one grain of truth in our belief that there is a living God, Who holds us unutterably dear, Who is seeking in all things, and through all things, ever to lead us to the highest, to the fullest, to the best, what room is there for us to fret and fear?"

—Rev. Mark Guy Pearce.

"No longer need any soul feel Fatherless, for, to the request of Philip, 'Lord, show us the Father, and it sufficeth us', Jesus Himself has given the answer. 'He that hath seen ME hath seen the Father' (John xiv. 7-11). Blessed, indeed, are they who, by the acceptance of Jesus Christ as Saviour, have found God to be their Father."

—B.M'C.B.

"Need! yes, need! that is the thing which presses
    On every hand; in many forms as well:
Need! yes, need! 'tis that which much distresses
    Need which we deeply know, but may not tell.

Your Father knoweth! yes, minutely, kindly;
    Knoweth the need, whate'er its form may be
Knoweth and understandeth; nor yet blindly
    Doth He behold whate'er now presses thee.

'Your Father knoweth'—words He meant for healing
    Meant to relieve—to comfort, to assure;
Spoken with gracious tenderness and feeling
    Uttered to be for care its constant cure.

Lie back, O soul, on this word from the Master,
    E'en though to-day grave need seems pressing thee
He abides faithful: look not for disaster;
    God shall supply your need—whate'er it be."

(J. Danson Smith.)

PEACE—CHRIST'S GIFT

" Peace I leave with you, My peace I give unto you : not as the world giveth, give I unto you. Let not your heart be troubled, neither let it be afraid."—John xiv. 27.

" PEACE is Christ's peculiar gift to His people. He seldom gives them money, or worldly ease, or temporal prosperity. These are, at best, very questionable possessions. They often do more harm than good to the soul. They act as clogs and weights to our spiritual life. Inward peace of conscience, arising from a sense of pardoned sin and reconciliation with God, is a far greater blessing. This peace is the inheritance of all believers, whether high or low, rich or poor.

The peace which Christ gives He calls ' My peace.' It is specially His own to give, because He bought it by His own blood, purchased it by His own substitution, and is appointed by the Father to dispense it to a perishing world.

The peace that Christ gives is not given as the world gives. What He gives the world cannot give at all ; and what He gives is given neither unwillingly nor sparingly, nor for a little time. Christ is far more willing to give than man is to receive. What He gives, He gives to all eternity, and never takes away. He is ready to give abundantly, ' above all that we can ask or think.' ' Open thy mouth wide,' He says, ' and I will fill it ' (Eph. iii. 20 ; Psl. lxxxi. 10).

Who can wonder that a legacy like this should be backed by the renewed emphatic charge, ' Let not your heart be troubled, neither let it be afraid ! ' There is nothing lacking on Christ's part for our comfort, if we will only look by faith to the one true Saviour,—there is medicine for every trouble of heart. Half our doubts and fears arise from dim perceptions of the real nature of Christ's Gospel."—*Rev. J. C. Ryle, D.D.*

" Once I thought I walked with Jesus,
　　Yet such changeful moods I had ;
　Sometimes trusting, sometimes doubting,
　　Sometimes joyful, sometimes sad.

　For He called me closer to Him,
　　Bade my doubting tremors cease ;
　And when I had fully trusted—
　　Filled my soul with *perfect peace*.

　Oh, the peace my Saviour gives,
　　Peace I never knew before :
　For my way has brighter grown,
　　Since I learned to trust Him more."

　　　　　　　　　　　—F. A. Blackmer.

FEAR NOT!

God is omniscient and omnipotent

"What time I am afraid, I will trust in Thee."—Psalm lvi. 3.

"I will trust and not be afraid."—Isa. xii. 2.

WHEN I'm afraid of times before,
　　What coming days will bring,
When life's omissions I deplore,
　　And earth-mists round me cling;
O Lord of love, my weakness see—
When I'm afraid I'll trust in Thee.

When I'm afraid of wily foes,
　　Their flattery and hate—
Who seek my progress to oppose—
　　My joys to dissipate;
O Lord of hosts, my weakness see—
When I'm afraid I'll trust in Thee.

When I'm afraid of dangers near,
　　Foreboding future ills;
When rocks, and shoals, and deeps I fear,
　　And gloom my spirit fills;
O Lord of might, my weakness see—
When I'm afraid I'll trust in Thee.

When I'm afraid of crushing loss,
　　Parting from loved ones dear—
Lest I shall murmur at my cross,
　　And yield to faithless fear;
O Lord of peace, my weakness see—
When I'm afraid I'll trust in Thee.

When I'm afraid of failing health,
　　Sore weaknesses I know—
And illness steals o'er me by stealth,
　　And sickness lays me low;
O Lord of power, my weakness see—
When I'm afraid I'll trust in Thee.

When I'm afraid of drear old age,
　　As nature's powers decay—
Mortality's dread heritage,
　　Increasing day by day;
O Lord of grace, my weakness see—
When I'm afraid I'll trust in Thee.

—A. Gardner.

PEACE—BY CHRIST'S BLOOD

" It pleased the Father that in Him (Jesus) should all fulness dwell ; and, having made *peace* through the blood of His cross, by Him to reconcile all things unto Himself."
—Col. i. 19, 20.

" **G**OD made *peace* by blood. It is a very wonderful conception of redemption, which is presented to us in the New Testament. It is so wonderful to think that when all our world and race were at war with God— He, so far as He could, and at infinite cost, put out of the way the cause of hostility. But He could only do it at the cost of blood. I confess that I have no plumb-line to fathom all that is meant by making peace through the blood of the Cross. . . . But all we need to emphasize now is the fact that when God made peace it was based on righteousness, and the demands of righteousness were met at the cost of infinite suffering of which the emblem is shed blood.

If we are to make peace with men it will have to be at heavy cost to ourselves. If there is strife between ourselves and others, as we were once at war with God, it may be needful for us, at a great cost of tears and anguish, to remove from between them and us the obstacles to peace. It will cost us something to make and maintain peace. We shall have to sacrifice our pride, reputation, the maintenance of our fancied rights, to say nothing of ease and self-indulgence, if we shall repair the wrong of the evil-doer, and readjust broken relationships. The ambassadors of peace throughout the world have had to expend their very life blood in their endeavour to make peace, consistently with the demands of righteousness."

—*Rev. F. B. Meyer, D.D.*

" By Christ on the cross peace was made,
My debt by His death was all paid,
No other foundation is laid
For peace, the gift of God's love.

In Jesus for peace I abide,
And as I keep close to His side
There's nothing but peace doth betide,
Sweet peace ; the gift of God's love."

(*P. B. Bilhorn*).

FEAR NOT!

God is with us

"I will fear no evil: for Thou art with me."—Psalm xxiii. 4.

"IN the midst of these scenes of increasing distress and world-wide suffering, in the midst of the evil which is gathering faster and faster over an ungodly age, God's people may say in confidence, 'I will fear no evil, for Thou art with me'. We know that we are in His hands, that He loveth us, that He has prayed and still prays for all His own, that they should be kept from the evil (John xvii. 15). Judgment cannot reach us, for we are sheltered by His blood, and He has assured us that we have passed from death unto life, and shall not come into judgment (John v. 24). The great tribulation He announced to come at the close of this age is not for His own blood-bought people. Wrath is to come, but He tells us we are to be delivered from that wrath (I Thess. i. 10). In the midst of increasing distress and approaching evil we can say—'I will fear no evil.' And if that comes, which we call in our little life down here 'evil'—if loved ones are snatched away, if we lose earthly things and comforts, if suffering and sorrow come, we know that all these things must work together for our good. What a comfort! And so, beloved in the Lord, as we go through the year, a year whose end we may never see down here, let us say, 'I will fear no evil; for Thou art with me'. He is with us; and underneath are the everlasting arms; the arms which never fail; the arms which were outstretched upon Calvary's cross; the arms which uphold all things. Repeat it daily! Let it be the joyful song of faith in your soul and upon your lips, 'I will fear no evil; for Thou art with me'."

—Dr. A. C. Gaebelein.

Oh! haven blest of quietness
    Above earth's troubled roar—
Men's hearts are failing them for fear
    Mine never trembles more:
For I retire above with Him,
    Whose will does all restrain;
I know the wildest storms of earth
    Surge round that Rock in vain.

Thus, in His wisdom I can trust,
    Waiting, since He waits too:
Man's lawlessness but ripening
    Designs they never knew.
As when Golgotha's murderer
    Worked out God's deepest love,
Faith, understanding, learns to trust
    The heart that plans above."

(Anon.)

PEACE—THE SAVIOUR'S LEGACY

" The peace of God, which passeth all understanding, shall keep your hearts and minds through Christ Jesus."
—Philip. iv. 7.

"THE term ' the peace of God ' naturally includes, and is based upon, the reality of peace *with* God. It is only when we realize that, ' being justified by faith, we have peace with God ' (Rom. v. 1) that we can be assured of ' the peace of God ' of which the Apostle speaks. There is no other way to obtain the power that, like a garrison, will guard our inward being. We must first and foremost have accepted the substitutionary sacrifice of Christ as the means of our redemption, and have laid the whole burden of sin upon the Lamb of God before we can experience the blessing of peace. Then, when we have learned to rest upon the finished work of Christ, the burden of guilt is removed from the soul, and the ' peace that passeth all understanding ' becomes our inalienable privilege.

It is well to remember that this is the bequest of the Lord Jesus to His followers. He is ever standing in the midst of His disciples with the sweet benediction on His lips, ' Peace be unto you ' (John xx. 19-21). Still He speaks to those who know Him as their Saviour, their Teacher, their Friend, saying, ' My peace I give unto you ' (John xiv. 27). Not only for the few who were gathered with Him in the upper room were these words intended, but for all who have taken their stand upon His side, and are seeking to do His will and live to His praise, and we are missing an inestimable boon if we fail to lay claims to such a legacy."—*Rev. F. J. Horsefield.*

" The waves that break across the troubled ocean
  Are only on the surface ; there they cease,
For underneath no violent commotion
  Disturbs the calm and quietness of peace.

And when a tempest's fury is expended,
  The wide sea bears upon its placid breast
The waves whose war tumultuous is ended
  In quiet stillness and unruffled rest.

And thus the strife and agony of living
  Are on life's surface ; not a wave that rolls
Disturbs when Jesus, loving and forgiving,
  Commands His peace deep down in human souls.

No raging storm, however rough its riot,
  Invades the stillness of the innermost,
For there, supreme, prevails eternal quiet,
  The ' peace of Christ ' through God the Holy Ghost.

And when the storms of time are past and ended,
  The surface waves will leave no trace of strife.
The inward and the outward will be blended
  In calm, serene, unbroken, endless life."   (*F. W. Pitt.*)

FEAR NOT!
Trials bring Him near

"Cast thy burden upon the Lord, and He shall sustain thee."—Psalm lv. 22.

"'CAST thy *burden* on the Lord.' The margin says 'thy *gift*'. The burden becomes a gift, because, as the text itself suggests, it brings the Burden-bearer so near to us that we are enabled to cling to Him, while the arm of His strength sustains us. Trials bring the Saviour near: 'I will be with him in trouble'. When St. Paul stood unbefriended before Nero's judgment seat, the Lord stood by him and strengthened him. When the Psalmist-king entered the valley of the shadow of death, the Shepherd of Souls drew near, and walked with him step by step: 'Thou art with me', he exclaims, in serene trust. When Abraham, lonely and heart-sick with deferred hopes, cried passionately, 'Lord God what wilt thou give me?' the Lord answered, 'I will give thee Myself—Fear not, Abraham, I am thy shield and thy exceeding great reward.'

'Cast thy burden on the Lord, and He shall sustain thee.' 'Sustain' may seem to be a stately term, but it is just the word which Isaiah uses to describe the deliverances of the Exodus and the wilderness wandering—'He bare them and carried them all the days of old.' One may imagine the march to Marah and Elim after the Red Sea had been safely crossed, and the tribes had come into the liberty of the redeemed. Each family must carry its own equipment—the father, the mother, and the elder children, all take their share, each bearing his own burden. But the youngest, a little lad, begs to be allowed to 'do his bit'. A light load is laid upon his shoulders, and he goes forward gaily and proudly into the desert. But soon the sun pours its rays like spears upon the cavalcade: the torrid sand blisters the feet, and the poor little pilgrim is ready to faint. He slips his hot hand into the father's and *he* understands. Stooping down, he swings the child upon his shoulders, and carries him, and his burden, all the way, until they come to the camping ground where fresh waters sparkle, where the grass is green, where the palms cast their cool shadow, and where the evening breeze blows softly. 'Cast thy burden on the Lord, and He shall sustain thee:' He will bear *thee and thy burden*."

—*Rev. D. M. McIntyre, D.D.*

"So into His hand went mine,
And into my life came He:
And I walked with a joy divine
The path I had *feared* to see."

PEACE—GOD'S, WITHIN

" He is our peace."—Eph. ii. 14.

" The fruit of the Spirit is . . . peace."—Gal. v. 22.

" CHRIST is our peace. In Him God speaks pardon for our sins, because of His Death and Resurrection, and peace for life's daily lot by His indwelling. This means that as well as enjoying peace with God as a result of our reconciliation to Him,—we may know constantly the peace of God in all life's relationships and circumstances. In life's lot Paul knew much tumult, yet he could urge his fellow Christians to share his enjoyment of peace : ' Let the peace of God *rule* in your hearts ' (Col. iii. 15).

Perfect peace is the peace of God, and it is possible to be kept in such peace. To be thus kept is as though we were surrounded by a guard. In time of siege a city enjoys that measure of peace within its borders which is commensurate with the strength of the responsible garrison, and the confidence of the people in these defenders. In our daily lot, attacked, as we are, by our spiritual foes, we shall have the peace of God garrisoning our hearts and thoughts, according to our faith in our Keeper. ' The angel of the Lord encampeth round about them that fear Him, and delivereth them ' (Psl. xxxiv. 7).

The fruit of the Spirit is the tranquillity of mind, and perpetual calm of disposition, which is known by those who practise the habit of ' prayer and supplication with thanksgiving ' (Philip. iv. 6, 7). We sometimes say— it takes two to make a quarrel. Do we realize that it takes two to keep the peace. God is willing to preserve us in perfect peace ; but what of that, if we do not keep within His will, and fulfil the conditions of fellowship ?

Peace is so much the characteristic of God, that Paul calls Him, ' the God of Peace.' God Himself is the Home of the trusting heart. When we are stayed upon Him, we shall not be exempt from trouble or conflict in life. But we are assured of a perfectly peaceful heart amidst life's tumults, as a bird may have perfect refuge in the cleft of a rock, even when the raging storms beat around."

—Rev. Neil McLachlan.

FEAR NOT!

He has left us His Peace

"Let not your heart be troubled: ye believe in God, believe also in Me."—John xiv. 1-2.

"Peace I leave with you, My peace I give unto you . . . Let not your heart be troubled, neither let it be afraid."—John xiv. 27.

"TWICE, then, does Christ forbid the troubled heart. In His own peace, and without fear, He would have us always tread the way to the Father's house. And His words appear even more wonderful when we remember that they were originally spoken to those who were just entering the darkest shadow that ever fell athwart the path of men who hope in God. Let us be thankful that it was *just then* that Jesus did say, 'Let not your heart be troubled'. For, if He had said it in the morning sunshine, in the gloom and the darkness of night we should, possibly, have put away His words as unsuitable and inappropriate. Yes, it was when Judas was at the door, and when God was about to allow wicked hands to crucify His Son, and almost to appear to surrender the world to the domination of devils and malicious men—it was then that the Prince of Peace most beautifully brought forth the treasures of His peace and joy, and bade His own share them with Him to the full, and forever. So, no darkness in our circumstances and outlook can excuse the troubled heart."

—*The Christian Alliance.*

" 'See that ye be not troubled!'
It came with unwelcome news—
This word of the Blesséd Spirit,
Who best His own Word can use.

And so, on this strong Word resting,
We lived through the days in peace;
The ordeal was passed through safely,
And strength got a fresh increase."

—*J. Danson Smith.*

PEACE—ALREADY MADE

"Therefore being justified by faith, we have peace with God through our Lord Jesus Christ : by Whom also we have access by faith into this grace wherein we stand, and rejoice in hope of the glory of God."—Rom. v. 1, 2.

"LET us *have* peace. God has made it, now let us *take* it. Many persons are trying to make peace, but peace is already made through Jesus Christ, and all that God asks of us is to take the reconciliation that He offers, and *have* the peace He has arranged. Many persons are acting toward God as if He were at war with them, as if everything were against them, and God were their worst enemy. The truth is, God was in Christ reconciling the world unto Himself, and the death of Jesus was the outflow of His own personal and sovereign love, and when we see this and know it, we are ready to lay down our arms and become His friends.

After the old French war, it is said that a French frigate was seen flying from an English warship, in the Southern Seas. The British cruiser pursued the frigate, and after a hard chase overtook her. The Frenchman hauled up the white flag and surrendered, and as he presented his sword to his conqueror, the Englishman laughed at him, and asked what he meant by surrendering.

'Why,' he said, 'didn't you know the war was over, and peace has been made for months ? '

'Why, no,' said the Frenchman. 'I thought we were still at war and I tried to escape. When I could not, the only thing left for me was to surrender. But I have been so long away from civilized parts and the news of the world, that I did not even hear that peace was made.' The men cordially shook hands, the sword was given back to the brave Frenchman, and they sat down together as comrades. The war was over, and they said, 'Let us have peace,' because peace was at headquarters.

This is what God means. Peace is made for every man who will take it through Jesus Christ, turn from his sins and accept the Saviour as Redeemer and Lord. Don't try to please God by your own works, and earn His favour, but frankly accept His forgiveness, turn from your rebellion and disobedience, and accept the peace which has been sealed through the precious blood of Christ."

—Rev. A. B. Simpson, D.D.

FEAR NOT!

We are of value to Him

"Are not five sparrows sold for two farthings, and not one of them is forgotten before God."—Luke xii. 6.

"I'M only a little sparrow—
　　A bird of low degree;
My life is of little value,
　　But the dear Lord cares for me.

He gave me a coat of feathers—
　　It's very plain I know;
With never a speck of crimson,
　　For it was not made for show.

But it keeps me warm in winter,
　　And shields me from the rain;
Were it bordered with gold and purple,
　　Perhaps it would make me vain.

And now that the springtime cometh,
　　I will build me a little nest,
With many a chirp of pleasure,
　　In the spot I love the best.

I have no barn or storehouse,
　　I neither sow nor reap;
God gives me a sparrow's portion,
　　But never a seed to keep.

If my meat is sometimes scanty,
　　Close picking makes it sweet;
I have always enough to feed me,
　　And 'Life is more than meat'.

I know there are many sparrows—
　　All over the world they're found;
But our heavenly Father knoweth,
　　When one of us falls to the ground.

Though small we are never forgotten;
　　Though weak, we are never afraid;
For we know that the dear Lord keepeth
　　The life of the creatures He made.

I fly through the thickest forest,
　　I light on many a spray;
I have no chart or compass,
　　But I never lose my way.

I just fold my wings at nightfall,
　　Wherever I happen to be;
For the Father is always watching:
　　No harm can happen to me."

PEACE—BY RECONCILIATION

" Let him take hold of my strength, that he may make peace with Me ; and he shall make peace with Me."
—Isa. xxvii. 5.

" SUCH are the alternatives. You must either resist God's strength, or take hold of it. If the former, it is as though thorns and briers should resist flame. There is no fury in God ; He has no desire for the death of the ungodly, but that he should turn from his unrighteousness and live. Yet, if the blinded soul persists in flinging himself into collision with Him, it must suffer finally and irretrievably. But notice the double invitation, ' Let him take hold of My strength : let him make peace.'

' Where shall we find His strength ? ' the sinner asks. ' In the mighty mountains girded with strength ; in the arch of the sky ; in the break of the ocean wave ? ' No not in these ; but where that dying Man pours out His soul unto death, and is numbered with the transgressors. But surely *there* is the *weakness* of God, not the strength ! Nay, but it is the strength. The weakness of God is stronger than men. ' We preach Christ crucified : to the Jews a stumbling-block, and to the Greeks foolishness, but unto them which are called, Christ the power of God.'

Come hither, soul of man ; the strength of God is in that pierced, transfixed hand. Take hold of it, it will lift thee. In Him God is reconciled ; there is nothing to do but to take the offered mercy, accept His reconciliation, and *be at peace*. God is reconciled ; be thou reconciled. God has made peace ; be thou at peace. God reaches out His hand ; take hold of it. God draws nigh ; draw nigh to Him. Then He will keep thee, whatever be thy foes or temptations ; His protecting strength will interpose between them and thee. He will keep thee night and day."—*Rev. F. B. Meyer, D.D.*

" At peace with God ! How great the blessing.
In fellowship with Him to be ;
And from all stains of sin set free,
How rich am I such wealth possessing.

The fear of death has gone for ever
No more to cause my heart to grieve
There is a place, I do believe,
In heaven for me beyond the river.

At peace with God !—No change can harm me,
Which ever way my course may run ;
One wish alone—God's will be done
I seek since I have known His mercy.

My soul has found a resting place,
And I am now through heavenly grace,
At peace with God, at peace with God."

(*R. Slater.*)

FEAR NOT!

Nothing separates from His Love

"Perfect love casteth out fear."—I John iv. 18.
"He loved me, and gave Himself for me."—Gal. ii. 20.
"Who shall separate us from the love of Christ?"—Rom. viii. 35.

"HOW can we measure God's love? They say that a man's fist is the measure of his heart. Come and stand beneath the stars! There is God's hand! Now judge His heart! It is illimitable! By that love He has put our sins behind His back into the ocean depths! With that love He has drawn us out of the pit of our sins! By that love He bears with our cold response and languid petitions! Through that love He will bring us to glory! His is a love that will never let us go!

Are you oppressed with the sense of failure, with temptation, with the consciousness of sin? or oppressed with poverty or debt, or the fear of unemployment, or with inability to find work? Or cast down with bitter persecution within or without your home? Or sorely beset and hindered by ill-health, and the hopelessness of recovery? All these cases of oppression may be handed over to your faithful Creator, with the certainty that He is as willing, as He is able, to undertake for you. He is never weary of hearing your cry; the Everlasting Arms are never tired; and our God never slumbers nor sleeps.

Take the hand of Jesus to steady you: look down into the hole of the pit from which you have been redeemed, and then look up to the throne of God to which He passed at His Ascension, and recall His own words: 'Where I am, there shall ye be also'. Trust Him to undertake for your little life!"
—*Rev. F. B. Meyer, D.D.*

"I hear the words of love,
  I gaze upon the blood;
I see the mighty sacrifice,
  And I have peace with God.

'Tis everlasting peace—
  Sure as Jehovah's name;
'Tis stable as His stedfast throne,
  For evermore the same.

I change, He changes not:
  The Christ can never die:
His love, not mine, the resting place
  His truth, not mine, the tie."
(*Rev. Horatius Bonar, D.D.*)

PEACE—THROUGH HIS DEATH

"Having made peace through the blood of His Cross."
Col. i. 20.

"God forbid that I should glory, save in the cross of our Lord Jesus Christ, by Whom the world is crucified unto me, and I unto the world."—Gal. vi. 14.

"WE are coming to see, with ever-increasing clearness, that the only hope for mankind is to be found in the supreme sacrifice at Calvary. . . . We glory in the Cross with the deepest possible conviction, because it is the divine remedy for the tragedy of guilt. We are not ashamed to say that we believe in the Cross as an atonement for sin. We would be numbered among those who glory in the substitutionary death of our Lord Jesus Christ. We believe that He died for our sins; we accept the verdict of Holy Scripture, that He died on our behalf. He who knew no sin was made sin for us that we might be made the righteousness of God in Him (II Cor. v. 21). . . . There is no other hope for the world, and no other way of deliverance from the bondage of sin.

We shall never understand fully all that is included in the sufferings of our Lord Jesus Christ, but it is quite certain that He did not die the death of a martyr, nor did He die for His own sins: He offered Himself as a sacrifice for the world; and it is on the basis of that sacrifice that God is willing to be gracious to those who plead the all-prevailing Name. . . .

While we glory in the Cross, we glory, also, in the empty tomb. Our Saviour is alive for evermore. This is the simple faith of the Christian Church, and it is the Risen Christ Who, in the power of His Holy Spirit, applies to penitent hearts the healing virtues of His Cross and brings them into that condition before God where they are justified freely, and where it is possible for them no longer to walk after the flesh, but after the Spirit."
—*The Life of Faith*.

"On the Cross of Calvary,
Jesus died for you and me,
There He shed His precious blood,
That from sin we might be free.
There was full atonement made,
There my heavy debt was paid,
It was for me that Jesus died,
On the Cross of Calvary."

"Peace, perfect peace? in this dark world of sin!
The Blood of Jesus whispers peace within."
(*Bickersteth.*)

FEAR NOT!

He abideth faithful

**"He hath said, I will never leave thee, nor forsake thee."
—Heb. xiii. 5.**

"THERE are seasons, in the experience of many of God's people, when by reason of outward trials or inward troubles, they feel desolate and desponding. Spiritual comforts are gone. They have little of the hallowed communion they once enjoyed with their heavenly Father, little fervour or filial nearness in prayer —little pleasure in reading the Word or attending the sanctuary. A chilling blight has passed over their spiritual being. In the bitterness of conscious estrangement from the God of their life, they are led to harbour the secret thought—'The Lord hath forsaken me, and my God hath forgotten me.'. . . . Think of this. If His dealings should at times appear inexplicable—if, amid baffling dispensations, we may be led at times to say, with Gideon of old, 'If the Lord be with us, why is all this befallen us?' —let us hush the unkind misgiving, by the remembrance that the affection of the fondest human parent to her offspring is but a feeble shadow compared to that of Him Who pities as a father, comforts as a mother, and loves as God alone can do. . . . Go, burdened one, *fearlessly* on. 'He hath said, I will never leave thee nor forsake thee.' That loving eye never slumbers—that wakeful vigilance is never suspended. Dishonour not God by unbelieving distrust of His Words and ways. Look back on the past —trace His footprints of love—the unmistakable tokens of His presence and supporting grace, let these be encouragements for the present and pledges for the future. The dearest earthly friend may forget you—distance may sever—memory may fail—the mind may become a blank —the old familiar greetings may be met only by an unconscious gaze—Death *may* have already, and at some time will, put his impressive seal on the most sacred interchanges of human affection—'Yet will I not forget thee.' "   *Rev. J. R. Macduff, D.D.*

"God ever cares! And time can never change Him;
 His nature is to care, and love, and bless;
And dreariest, darkest, emptiest days afford Him
 But means to make more sweet His own caress."
                        —*J. Danson Smith.*

PEACE—THROUGH KINGSHIP

" Where is He that is born King ? "—Matt. ii. 2.

" The Prince of Peace."—Isa. ix. 6.

" He is our Peace."—Eph. ii. 14.

" The government shall be upon His shoulder."—Isa. ix. 6.

" WHERE is He that is born King ? ' is a question which we may profitably put to ourselves. For, too often, alas, even by those who profess to believe and serve Him, He is denied the throne. Men are not unwilling to accept His grace, if that can be done without yielding to His government. They are glad to have Him near to the precincts of life, in case they should come to need Him, but they will not allow Him its presidency, in case He should come to need them ! Indeed, the common cause of the powerlessness and ineffectiveness of so much avowed Christian life to-day is to be sought in the failure to recognize Christ as King, and to realize His unquestioned control. For, when ' His Kingdom ruleth over all,' life is invested with the sanctifying power which increasingly delivers it from all that is sordid and unworthy in motive and aim ; and at the same time inspires to self-forgetful service.

But, when He is not so enthroned, life's course runs on to increasing weakness and worthlessness, and its true end is lost. The gold, frankincense, and myrrh, lovingly bestowed upon Him, are strangely multiplied to the enrichment of the worshipper, as well as to the service of the Saviour. But, selfishly withheld from Him, they become a positive impoverishment. His enthronement conditions our moral and spiritual enduement ; and hence, no consideration can be quite so important as this present one—' Where is He that is born King ? ' "

—*Rev. J. Stuart Holden, D.D.*

" Jesus, my soul's victorious King,
  Thee I with joy proclaim ;
I yield me to Thy blesséd will ;
  I own Thy sovereign claim
O'er all I am, and all I have,
  To glorify Thy Name.

For Thou did'st stoop, dear Lord, to take
  Sin's heavy load from me ;
My King His glory laid aside,
  For lowliest ministry ;
And all my life to Him belongs
  Whose love hath set me free."

(*Fanny Forsaith.*)

FEAR NOT!

His presence is abiding

"Be strong and of a good courage . . . the Lord thy God is with thee whithersoever thou goest."—Josh. i. 9.

"Lo, I am with you alway, even to the end of the age."
—Matt. xxviii. 20.

" 'IT is the word of a gentleman, of the most strict and sacred honour, so there's an end of it!' says Livingstone to himself, as he places his finger for the thousandth time on the text on which he stakes his life. He is surrounded by hostile and infuriated savages. During the sixteen years that he has spent in Africa, he has never before seemed in such imminent peril. Death stares him in the face. He thinks sadly of his life-work scarcely begun. For the first time in his experience he is tempted to steal away under cover of the darkness, and to seek safety in flight. He prays! 'Leave me not, forsake me not,' he cries. But let me quote from his own journal: it will give us the rest of the story. 'January 14, 1856. *Evening.* Felt much turmoil of spirit in prospect of having all my plans for the welfare of this great region, and this teeming population, knocked on the head by savages to-morrow. But I read that Jesus said: "All power is given unto Me in heaven and in earth. Go ye therefore, and teach all nations, and *lo, I am with you alway, even unto the end of the world.*" It is the word of a gentleman, of the most strict and sacred honour, so there's an end of it! I will not cross furtively to-night as I intended. Should such a man as I flee? Nay, verily, I shall take observations for latitude and longitude to-night, though they be the last. *I feel quite calm now, thank God. . . .* Would you like me to tell you what supported me through all the years of exile among people whose language I could not understand, and whose attitude toward me was always uncertain and often hostile? It was this: "*Lo, I* am with you alway, even unto the end of the world*". On these words I staked everything, and they never failed!' "

—*Rev. F. W. Boreham, D.D.*

"He faileth not, nor ever groweth weary—
    The Mighty One, whose arm is strong to save
He giveth strength to aid the fainting pilgrim,
    And to the weak the courage to be brave.

He faileth not; His faithfulness abideth;
    Our friends may fail, but He remaineth true.
His 'Fear Nots' glow with comfort for the troubled
    The Faithful Guide will lead the journey through."

(*Rev. H. V. Andrews.*)

PEACE—THROUGH PRAYER

" Be careful for nothing ; but in everything by prayer and supplication with thanksgiving let your requests be made known unto God. And the peace of God, which passeth all understanding, shall keep your hearts and minds through Christ Jesus."—Phil. iv. 6, 7.

" 'IN everything,' be the matter utterly trivial or highly important, not one thing to be excluded from this range. The promise of perfect peace, is not made to any man who selects *portions* of his life for God's management, while he himself elects to control the remainder. God is very particular ; and, if His promise is to be literally fulfilled, His commands must be literally obeyed. The sixth verse means in one sentence : keep open heart with God. The man who lives in its spirit will refer everything to God, as naturally and easily as a little child consults its parents about the veriest trifles of its life. It will not occur to him to do anything else. He has sought the kingdom of God *first*, and he knows that the rest will, according to the promise, be ' added.' It is quite evident, then, in face of the promise, that whoever lives this simple life of ' faith on the Son of God,' treating God, not as an occasional house of refreshment, but as his ' habitation,' can have no room in the soul for worry."
—*Rev. F. C. Spurr.*

" What a friend we have in Jesus,
    All our sins and griefs to bear ;
What a privilege to carry
    Everything to God in prayer.
Oh, what *peace* we often forfeit,
    Oh, what needless pain we bear—
All because we do not carry
    Everything to God in prayer.

Are we weak and heavy laden,
    Cumbered with a load of care ?
Precious Saviour, still our refuge,—
    Take it to the Lord in prayer.
Do thy friends despise, forsake thee ?
    Take it to the Lord in prayer ;
In His arms He'll take and shield thee,
    Thou wilt find a solace there."
(*Joseph Scriven.*)

FEAR NOT!

Ponder the word "Father"

"Let not your heart be troubled; believe in God, believe also in Me."—John xiv. 1 (R.V. margin).

"JESUS is always an encourager, a minister of cheer. . . . If we would be comforters like our Master, we must inspire others to endurance. We must bring them something that will make them stronger. Mere condolence will not do it. We must have something to give which will impart strength and courage. What is there in the Gospel of Christ that gives us authority to say, 'Let not your heart be troubled'? The first thing Jesus bade his disciples do was to believe—'Believe in God, believe also in Me.' Thus far they had believed. Jesus had taught them a new name for God. They were to call Him 'Father'. He used almost no other name for God. The word 'Father' is a great treasure-house of love-thoughts. It told the disciples of the minute thought and care of God, extending to the smallest events of their lives. It told them of goodness that never failed. It was a great lesson they were learning—to think of God as their Father. In the shock of the last terrible days, however, there was danger that they would lose their faith. Yet, Jesus said in that dark hour: 'Believe in God. Let nothing take away from you your faith in God as your Father. . . .'

We are always in danger of losing our faith in times of trouble. Many people are heard asking such questions as, 'How can God be a God of love, and suffer me to be so bereft, so stripped of good?' 'Where now are the promises of blessing which are made so constantly in the Scriptures?' 'Has God forgotten to be gracious?' To such questions the answer is, 'Believe in God, believe also in Me'. Let nothing disturb your faith. Though it seems that love has failed, that God has forgotten you, that Christ is no longer your friend, still believe. Believe in God, believe also in Jesus Christ."

—Rev. J. R. Miller, D.D.

"Absolutely tender!
Absolutely true!
Understanding all things;
Understanding you!
Infinitely loving—
Intimately near!
This is GOD OUR FATHER
What have we to fear?"

(F.M.N.)

PEACE—IN BELIEVING

" Therefore being justified by faith, we have peace with God through our Lord Jesus Christ."—Rom. v. 1.

" Being justified freely by His grace through the redemption that is in Christ Jesus."—Rom. iii. 24.

" Now the God of Hope fill you with all joy and peace in believing."—Rom. xv. 13.

" ' **B**EING justified '—the natural consequence is peace. ' Just as Christian came up with the Cross, his burden loosed from off his shoulders, and fell from off his back and began to tumble, and so continued to do till it came to the mouth of the Sepulchre, where it fell in and I saw it no more. As he stood looking and weeping, behold three Shining Ones came to him and saluted him with, Peace be to thee. Then Christian gave three leaps for joy and went out singing :—

Blest Cross ! blest Sepulchre, blest rather be
The Man that there was put to shame for me.

Justification by faith gives immediate peace. In Korea, during the troubles of the Independent Movement, when many were imprisoned or killed for expressing their opinions, a girl prisoner wrote : ' After more than a month of sitting in an uncomfortable position, with absolutely nothing to read, no one to speak to, nothing to see, I received, with joy unspeakable, a copy of the New Testament in my own tongue. I read it through in two and a half days, then read it again. I felt as if I were standing beneath the Cross . . . all my troubles were gone ; and His peace was in my heart. Oh, how sweet it is to trust the Lord ! No matter what comes to my life, even though death comes to me, I shall be happy and at peace.' "

—Christine I. Tinling.

" Trusting in Jesus my Saviour divine,
I have the witness that still He is mine ;
Great are the blessings He giveth to me,
Oh, I am happy as mortal can be.

Once I was far from my Saviour and King ;
Now He has taught me His mercy to sing ;
Peace in believing He giveth to me,
Oh, I am happy as mortal can be.

Trusting in Jesus, oh, what should I fear ?
Nothing can harm me when He is so near !
Sweet is the promise He giveth to me :
Oh, I am happy as mortal can be."

FEAR NOT!

Might has its home within me

"God gave us not a spirit of fearfulness: but of power and love and discipline."—II Tim. i. 7 (R.V.).

"INSTEAD of fearfulness and shame—POWER. And the power is heaven-born and heaven-sustained, bequeathed and nourished by the Spirit of God. What opposition should I dread, from what enemy should I fly, when this invincible Might has its home within me? My weakness, leaning upon God, its end can never miss. He delights in the empty and helpless soul into which He can breathe His strength.

Instead of fearfulness and shame—LOVE. The very love of Jesus, limitless, unconquerable towards men who range themselves against His gospel. If this love abounds in me, it will drive terror far away. It will make me the envoy of peace to those who hate me. Above all, my shrinking from them will rise and reign a throbbing compassion for them. Stronger than my misgivings of the harm they may inflict on me, will be my knowledge of the sorrowful destiny they may reap for themselves—my yearning to snatch them from it.

Instead of fearfulness and shame—DISCIPLINE. The sober and continual government of my self: the watchfulness that mounts even into prayer. Let me have this lordship over my frailties, my alarms, my moods of despondency and panic, and thrice am I armed: no shaft shall pierce my coat of mail.

> 'I fear no breathing bowman,
> But only, east or west,
> The awful other foeman
> Impowered in my breast.'

God, let me remember, gives me not a spirit of fearfulness, but of Power and Love and Discipline."
> —*Rev. Alexander Smellie, D.D.*

> "But I look up—into the face of Jesus,
> For there my heart can rest, my fears are stilled;
> And there is joy, and love, and light for darkness,
> And perfect peace, and every hope fulfilled."
> —*Selected.*

PEACE—THROUGH OBEDIENCE

" Great Peace have they which love Thy Law : and nothing shall offend (stumble) them."—Psl. cxix. 165.

" WHAT a charming verse is this ! It deals not with those who perfectly keep the law, for where should such men be found ?—but with those who love it,—whose hearts and hands are made to square with its precepts and demands. These men are ever striving, with all their hearts, to walk in obedience to the law, and though they are often persecuted, they have peace, yea, *great peace* ; for they have learned the secret of the reconciling blood ; they have felt the power of the comforting Spirit ; and they stand before the Father as men accepted. The Lord has given them to feel His peace, which passeth all understanding. They have many troubles, and are likely to be persecuted by the proud, but their usual condition is that of deep calm—a peace too great for this little world to break. ' *And nothing shall offend them,*' or, ' shall really injure them.' ' All things work together for good to them that love God, to them who are the called according to His purpose.' It must needs be that offences come, but these lovers of the law are peacemakers, and so they neither give nor take offence. That peace which is founded upon conformity to God's will is a living and lasting one, worth writing of with enthusiasm, as the Psalmist here does."

—Rev. C. H. Spurgeon.

" Open Thy Word of Truth,
　That I may see
Thy message written clear
　And plain for me ;
Then in sweet fellowship
　Walking with Thee,
Thine image on my life
　Engraved will be.

Bless Thou the Truth, dear Lord,
　To me, to me,
As Thou did'st bless the bread
　By Galilee :
Then shall all bondage cease,
　All fetters fall ;
And I shall find my *peace*,
　My all in all."

(Mary A. Lathbury.)

FEAR NOT!

His presence turns evil into Good

"Wherefore should I fear in the days of evil."—Psalm xlix. 5.

"HAVE I not God? At sundry times, and in divers manners, He spake to, and succoured His saints. Will He not come to me, and cast around me the soft mantle of His protecting love? And if I love Him, do I need any beside? Did He not walk with Enoch, and then take him home, before the deluge came? Did He not shut Noah in, with His own hand, that there should be no jeopardy from the overflowing flood? Did He not assure Abram that He was his shield and exceeding great reward, quieting his fears against any possible combination of foes? Did He not preserve His servant, Moses, from the fury of Pharaoh and the murmurings of Israel? Was not Elijah hidden in the secret of His pavilion from the wrath of Ahab? Did He not send His angel to shut the lions' mouths that they might not hurt Daniel? Were not the coals of the burning fiery furnace as sweet and soft as forest glades to the feet of the three young confessors? Has God ever forsaken those that trusted Him? Has He ever given them over to the will of their enemies?

Wherefore then should *I* fear in the day of evil? I may be standing on the deck, whilst the ship is beset by icebergs and jagged splintered rocks; the fog drapes everything, as the way slowly opens through this archipelago of peril; but God is at the helm—why should I fear? Days of evil to others cannot be so to me, for the presence of God transmutes the evil to good."

—*Rev. F. B. Meyer, D.D.*

God is for me! Soul of mine, believe it!
God is for me, always, ever, now;
God is for me—'tis His own blest statement
Soul of mine, oh, worshipfully bow.

God is for me when life's skies are sunny;
For me just the same when clouds o'ercast
For me—never would He be against me—
For me, ever for me, to the last.

God is for me! Forces are against me;
Unseen powers of darkness may oppose.
God is for me! Sovereign! Lord! Almighty!
Vanquisher of all His children's foes.

God is for me! Yes, I will believe it!
Stay my heart on His unchanging Word
Darkest days may help me but to prove it:
God is for me! loving, sovereign, Lord.

(*J. Danson Smith.*)

PEACE—THROUGH SUBMISSION

" Be careful for nothing ; but in everything by prayer and supplication with thanksgiving let your requests be made known unto God. And the peace of God, which passeth all understanding, shall keep your hearts and minds through Christ Jesus."—Phil. iv. 6, 7.

" PEACE is possible to every believer in Christ. No Christian can say, ' That is very beautiful. It shines in my friend's face like heaven's radiance. But it is not for me.' The peace of God is for every believer. God shows no favouritism in dispensing this blessing. There is great diversity in the natural gifts and abilities bestowed upon individuals. . . But in grace the best is open to all. The divine peace is not for a few : it is a blessing which all may obtain. No matter how restless, how turbulent, how full of care, how naturally given to worry and anxiety, one may be, this sweet, quiet, restful peace of God is possible of attainment. Yet there are a great many good people who have not yet learned the secret of peace. . . . Their lives are full of little anxieties. They are easily annoyed. Their faces show lines of care and fret. Now and then they have brief seasons of restful trust, when they seem to have gotten the victory, but, in a little time, they are back again in the old broken restlessness. This is not the best that Christ can do for us. . . . It is very evident that this life of peace is not a life without care. Christ nowhere suggests the thought that his disciples are lifted out of the common conditions of earthly life into a sheltered pilgrimage, where the storms do not beat upon them. . . . Nor is it by dulling the sensibilities that Christ gives peace. It is a peace in the heart which He gives, a peace which one may have within while without storms are raging ; a calm in the soul in the midst of external agitations and tumults ; a spirit unperturbed, unfretted, unruffled in the midst of life's multitudinous cares. . . . What then shall we do with the things that would naturally worry us ? St. Paul tells us, ' In nothing be anxious, but in everything by prayer and supplication with thanksgiving, let your requests be made known unto God.' That is, instead of being fretted and distracted over the things which we cannot control, we are to put them out of our hands into God's by specific prayer, and leave them there.

Is not the lesson worth learning at any cost ? It can be learned ; it has been learned. Its one secret is perfect submission to the will of God. Every resistance or disobedience causes unrest and sorrow ; but quiet acceptance, with loving confidence and joyous song, will bring the peace of God into the soul."—*Rev. J. R. Miller, D.D.*

FEAR NOT!

Our very present help

"God is our refuge and strength, a very present help in trouble. Therefore will not we fear, though the earth be removed, and though the mountains be carried into the midst of the sea."—Psalm xlvi. 1-2.

" ' A VERY present Help' in Thee
    Our souls have often found,
And now again to Thee we turn,
    As troubles close us round.

We look upon the warring world,
    Where only strife appears,
And from its desolation drear
    No ray the spirit cheers.

We see the heart of fallen man
    Revealed in hideous sin;
The wrath of man let loose to blight
    The world Christ died to win.

We look above, and lo! we see
    Omnipotent to-day
The King enthroned, Whose Kingdom blest
    Shall never pass away.

And as we gaze, His words we hear,
    'All power is given to Me,'
And peace steals on the troubled heart—
    The Lord our Strength will be.

We know not what the days may bring,
    Nor what we must endure,
But *we know Him*, Whose truth is pledged
    To be our Refuge sure.

Then calm amid surrounding fears,
    Lord, let Thy servants be;
To glorify Thee by a peace
    Which springs from trust in Thee.

To guide the weary feet around
    Into the path of life,
To find that promised rest of soul
    Amid the earthly strife.

Yea, Lord, 'a present Help' Thou art,
    Oh, may we show again
That those who put their trust in Thee
    Shall never trust in vain."

                —*Freda Hanbury Allen.*

PEACE—ITS PERMANENCE

" Ye shall . . . be led forth with peace."—Isa. lv. 12.

" How beautiful are the feet of them that preach the Gospel of Peace, and bring glad tidings of good things."—Rom. x. 15.

" PEACE, such as God gives, is not destroyed even amidst the heaviest storms ; and see how it avails under the *common* circumstances of life ! What is it that gives real abiding cheerfulness to the day ? What is it that makes the task so easy, the labour so light? What is it that spreads itself all around as a tranquil atmosphere. What is it,—but the influence of peace ? And it has a blessed effect upon others ; there is nothing that wins men, nothing that sooner leads them to inquire into the nature and power of the Gospel of Peace, than seeing peace manifested in the life, peace written on the very countenance of the holy. What good it does, too, to beginners, to those just setting out on their Christian course, when they thus learn how great a present blessing is within their own reach ! And yet, as none can quite penetrate those depths of the heart where peace dwells, none can see in others a thousandth part of the blessing as it lies there ; or perceive, if they have not themselves experienced it, how truly it is called ' the peace of God that passeth all understanding.' Indeed, how can it be understood ? Is it not a mystery to a man's own self ? In the midst of the many hopes and fears, doubts and distresses, that are often in the heart, how wonderful it is that, on the whole, there is peace there—peace, like some rock that the heaving and surging waves hide for a moment from the eye, but which yet abides fixed and unshaken for ever."—*Rev. T. V. Fosbery, M.A.*

> " My mind is stayed on Thee,
> O God, my Strength, my Rock;
> Thou art a rallying-place for me
> 'Mid storm and strain and shock.
>
> And Thou wilt keep in peace,
> So perfect, so sublime,
> That nerves shall quieten, tension cease,
> In every troubled time.
>
> The sailor ' stays ' his mast
> On strongest ropes there be ;
> Thus, Lord, my soul, by Thee held fast,
> Doth stay herself on Thee.
>
> The workman ' stays ' with wires
> Fixed in some root of tree—
> The swaying pole that grip requires—
> So stays my mind on Thee.
>
> This attitude is mine !
> Then Thou art pledged to keep
> Without my cry, or prayer, or sign,
> In peace divinely deep."　　*(Winifred A. Iverson.)*

FEAR NOT!

Believers have no right to fear

"Fear hath torment."—I John iv. 18.
"I will trust and not be afraid."—Isa. xii. 2.

" 'FEAR NOT' is the water mark of the Word of God from the Pentateuch, the historical books, and the Psalms, through the Prophets, the Gospels, the Epistles and the Revelation.

Yet mothers say, 'I'm so afraid our children will have the chicken pox!' Housewives say, 'I'm afraid my canned goods will spoil!' Fathers say, 'I'm afraid I shall lose my job, and we shall starve'. Travellers (Christians all these) say, 'I'm afraid of aeroplanes, subways, lightning or what not'. Farmers say, 'I'm afraid we'll have frost early and ruin my crop'.

But no believer in the Lord Jesus Christ has any right or reason to fear anything or anyone on the earth or under it. When a Christian woman first appropriated, 'What time I am afraid, I will trust in Thee' (Psalm lvi. 3), she got pulled up with spiritual pride, but was quickly deflated when she read that D. L. Moody had said that this verse was going to heaven by second class; but 'I will trust and not be afraid' (Isa. xii. 2) was going to heaven by first class."

"There is a heart, there is a hand, we feel but cannot see;
We've always been provided for, and we shall always be.

He Who hath led will lead, all through the wilderness:
He Who hath fed will feed: He Who hath blessed will bless.

"Casting all your care on Him, casting all your care on Him
He will joy and blessing bestow,
When you cast all your care on Him."

"Say not, my soul, 'From whence
Can God relieve thy care?'
Remember that Omnipotence
Hath servants everywhere."

"Faith came singing into my room,
And other guests took flight:
Fear and Anxiety, Grief and Gloom
Sped out into the night.

I wondered that such things could be,
But Faith said gently, 'Don't you see
They really cannot live with me?' "

"Have we God's own 'Fear not' in our heart and life?"

—*The Sunday School Times.*

PEACE—ITS INFLUENCE

"If it be possible, as much as lieth in you, live peaceably with all men."—Rom. xii. 18.

"With God all things are possible."—Mark x. 27.

"Blessed are the peacemakers : for they shall be called the children of God."—Matt. v. 9.

"SOME have so drunk in the spirit of the great Peace-maker, that you may say of them, *they are in the world reconciling.* Their acts, words, characters, all emit an influence of healing peace. Blessed are all classes of these Christ-like souls !

For instance, there are such, not perhaps endued with the weight of character to compose a quarrel, but still full of the ardent affections that are very potent in preventing quarrels arising. There are lives so affluent in friendships that they link multitudes of other lives together. There are generous natures, contact with whom always leaves you with a better estimate of your fellowmen ; some who never feel a flame of ill-feeling ; some have the faithfulness to give the good report of those disliked, and go through life making no enemies, but many friends. In their lips the estranging sarcasm is not found, and in their hearts a cold indifference has no home. Some souls are so bright, and diffuse so much delight, that contention is kept out by joy. They are too loving to be scornful, or impatient, or unfair ; not ready to ' take up ' an ill report ; so good that they easily believe in goodness ; so self-forgetful that injuries, unpleasant words, or unkindly acts take no root in their memory, and no grudge ever rises in their heart.

These peacekeepers are peacemakers ; and, if any in this world are blessed, it is those that help to bind their fellows to each other in bonds of mutual affection and esteem."

—*Richard Glover.*

" The bread that giveth strength I want to give
The water pure that bids the thirsty live ;
I want to help the fainting day by day,
Because I shall not pass again this way.
I want to give the oil of joy for tears ;
The faith to conquer cruel doubts and fears
Beauty for ashes may I give alway,
Because I shall not pass again this way.
I want to give good measure running o'er
And into angry hearts I want to pour
The answer soft that turneth wrath away
Because I shall not pass again this way.
I want to give to others hope and faith ;
I want to do all that the Master saith ;
I want to live aright from day to day,
Because I shall not pass again this way."

(*Anon.*)

FEAR NOT!

God promises quietness from fear

"Whoso hearkeneth unto Me shall dwell safely, and shall be quiet from fear of evil."—Prov. i. 33.

"WISDOM speaks thus. Wisdom is none other than our Lord. 'Wisdom crieth without; she uttereth her voice in the streets . . . turn ye at my reproof; behold, I will pour out My Spirit unto you, I will make known My Words unto you' (Prov. i. 20-23). And He promises safety, and quietness from fear and evil, for all who hearken unto Him and are obedient unto His Word. 'The righteous shall be in everlasting remembrance. He shall not be afraid of evil tidings: his heart is fixed, trusting in the Lord' (Psalm cxii. 6, 7). These and similar words given to us who know the Lord may now be tasted in all their sweet blessedness. Thanks be to the God of all comfort, for the comfort wherewith He comforteth us. That able man of God, Charles H. Spurgeon, wrote years ago, the following, which is worthy to be passed on at this time: 'Divine love is rendered conspicuous when it shines in the midst of judgments. Fair as the lone star which smiles through the rifts of the thunder clouds: bright as the oasis which blooms in the wilderness of sand: so fair and so bright is love in the midst of wrath. When the Israelites provoked the Most High by their continued idolatry, He punished them by withholding both dew and rain, so that their land was visited by a sore famine; but, while He did this, He took care that His own chosen ones should be secure. If all other brooks are dry, yet shall there be one reserved for Elijah; and when that fails, God shall still preserve for him a place of sustenance: nay, not only so, the Lord hath not simply one Elijah, but He hath a remnant, according to the election of grace, who were hidden by fifties in a cave, and though the whole land was subject to famine, yet these fifties in the cave were fed, from Ahab's table too, by his faithful, God-fearing steward, Obadiah. Let us draw from this the inference that, come what may, God's people are safe. Let convulsions shake the whole earth, let the skies themselves be rent in twain, yet amid the wreck of worlds, the believer shall be as secure as in the calmest hour of rest.' "

—A. C. Gaebelein.

"Stayed upon Jehovah, hearts are fully blest,
Finding as He promised, perfect peace and rest."

PEACE—THAT PASSETH UNDERSTANDING

" Now the God of Peace be with you all."—Rom. xv. 33.

" WE all need peace ! There are sources of peace which are common to all men. The peace of a happy home ; of an increasing business and enlarging influence ; of the respect and love of our fellows. . . . We can all understand a peace like that. But there is a ' peace that passeth understanding.' It is too deep for words. It is like the pillowed depths of the ocean, which are undisturbed by the passing storm. Here is a sufferer, almost always in acute pain, and needing constant attention, and yet so happy. Joy and Peace, like guardian angels, sit beside that bedside,—how do you account for it ? Let the sceptic and the scoffer answer ! Here is a peace that passeth understanding, which comes from the God of Peace.

For the Christian soul there is a silver lining in every cloud ; a blue patch in the darkest sky ; a turn in the longest lane ; a mountain view which shall compensate the steepest ascent. Wait on the Lord, and keep His way, and He shall exalt thee to inherit the land. The thing impossible shall be, because all things are possible to God.

The peace of God is the peace of the Divine Nature—the very tranquillity which prevails in the heart of the God of Peace. It was of this that Jesus spoke when He said, ' My peace I give unto you ' : for His own being was filled and blessed with it during His earthly career. ' The Lord of Peace Himself give you peace always.'

There are three things against which we must ever be on our guard lest they rob us of our peace. First, unconfessed sin ; second, worry ; third, the permission of an unrebuked selfish principle. The Apostle says, ' Let the Peace of God rule in your hearts.' The Greek word means arbitrate. Let God's Peace act as umpire. We shall not escape life's discipline. We may expect to abound here, and to be abased there. But amid all, God's Peace, like a white-winged sentinel angel, shall come down to garrison our heart with its affections, and our mind with its thoughts."—*Rev. F. B. Meyer, D.D.*

" I've yielded to God and I'm saved every hour,
I've yielded to God and I feel His sweet power,
I've trusted His promises, not one has failed,
Of all His good word though the tempter assailed.
Sweet, quiet, yielded life, blessed rest from all storm and
    strife,
God's own peace now fills my soul, as on Him my way I
    roll."   (*J. M. Kirk.*)

FEAR NOT!

Some things feared never happen

"Take . . . no thought for the morrow. . . . Sufficient
unto the day is the evil thereof."—Matt. vi. 34.

THE STREAM THAT IS NEVER CROSSED

"THERE'S many a sorrow and pain I know,
　　As we tread the path of life;
There's many a grief and lasting woe,
　　And the way is toil and strife.
But the hardest load we have to bear
　　Is the labour and strength that's lost
In building the bridge with toilsome care
　　O'er the stream that is never crossed.

We have fretting and worry from morn till night,
　　And anguish weighs on the heart—
The thorny way seems hard to right,
　　And life is a bitter part.
But there is a burden greater yet,
　　Much peace of soul it has cost,
It is building a bridge with toil and sweat,
　　O'er the stream that is never crossed.

There's looking for crossings all the day,
　　And searching along the shore
For a bridge or ford along the way
　　We shall never travel o'er.
There's sighing for useless toys in vain,
　　And dreaming of chances lost;
But 'tis hardest to bridge with might and main
　　The stream that is never crossed.

Then gather the roses along the way,
　　And treasure the fragrance rare;
Rejoice in the bright and joyous day,
　　Refusing to borrow care.
For sorrow and pain will surely come,
　　And your soul be tried and tossed;
But don't be bridging to reach your home
　　O'er the stream that is never crossed."

　　　　　　　　　　　　—A. Owen Larrison.

PEACE—AN ABIDING SHELTER

" Thou wilt keep him in perfect peace, whose mind is stayed on Thee : because he trusteth in Thee."—Isa. xxvi. 3.

"HERE is the divine remedy for peace in the midst of doubt, darkness, disturbance, depression, disaster and despair—'perfect peace, whose mind is stayed on Thee.' It adds immensely to the meaning of this verse, if we read it in its free translation : ' Thou wilt keep him in perfect peace, whose mind *stops at God*.' In other words, the mind that reckons on God in everything, and refuses to go beyond Him—the heart that is satisfied to lean hard upon Him, and to leave all its affairs to His almighty wisdom, love, and care—the heart that is stayed upon God—is kept in perfect peace.

Here, then, is an ever open, never-failing harbour of refuge for the sinking spirit ; for the exhausted frame ; for the troubled mind ; for the fearful and foreboding soul. Here is a ' shelter in the time of storm.'

' Not a surge of worry, not a shade of care,
Not a blast of hurry touch the spirit *there*.'

' THERE,' oh, soul, have you got ' there ' ? For it is only ' there ' that we find this peace that soothes and strengthens, that subdues, and sweetens, and sustains. Art thou so right with God that thou canst ' stay ' upon Him ; that thou canst ' stop at God,' unloading every care and leaving all in His all-loving hands ? It is only ' there ' that we can find perfect peace.

When the way is barred, and the future black,—stop thou at God. Go no further—not a single step. Concentrate on HIM. Abide in HIM. Wait on HIM. Be occupied with HIM. Praise HIM. Rejoice in HIM. Extol HIM. Commit your cause to HIM. Lean hard—lie back on HIM. The result is sure :—' The peace of God, which passeth all understanding, shall keep your hearts and minds through Christ Jesus ' (Philp. iv. 7)."

—B. McCall Barbour.

"Like a river glorious is God's perfect peace,
Over all victorious in its bright increase.
Perfect —yet it floweth fuller every day ;
Perfect—yet it groweth deeper all the way.

Hidden in the hollow of His blessèd hand
Never foe can follow, never traitor stand.
Not a surge of worry, not a shade of care,
Not a blast of hurry touch the spirit there.

Stayed upon Jehovah, hearts are fully blest,
Finding, as He promised, perfect peace and rest."
(Frances Ridley Havergal.)

FEAR NOT!

Fear is never from God

"Fear thou not; for I am with thee: be not dismayed; for I am thy God: I will strengthen thee; yea, I will help thee; yea, I will uphold thee with the right hand of my righteousness."—Isa. xli. 10.

"God hath not given us the spirit of fear; but of power, and of love, and of a sound mind."—II Tim. i. 7.

"FEAR, then, is *not from God*! Acknowledge this fact, and refuse to take it from the Devil, whose object is to destroy us by its power. Instantly and absolutely reject it.

Christ is the deliverer from fear. He delivers from all sorts of fear, at all times, in all places. He delivers NOW. It matters not from whence or what the fear may come; *if we are right with God*, it is our privilege to master and dispel it.

Miracles of physical restoration, recovery of mental balance, cessation of nervous excitement, healing of heart trouble, and supplies of spiritual power, would be experienced in countless weary, sad and broken lives, by the simple recognition of the fact that '*God hath not given us (His own) the spirit of fear*', and by our refusal to receive it from any other source.

What is there to fear? Since the past is under His blood (Col. i. 14), the present is protected by His power (I Pet. i. 5) and the future is provided and prepared for by His grace (Psalm xxiii. 6, John xiv. 1-3).

'Whoso hearkeneth unto ME shall dwell safely, and shall be quiet from fear of evil' (Prov. i. 33).

'Stand fast therefore in the liberty wherewith Christ hath made us free' (Gal. v. 1).

'Submit yourselves therefore to God. Resist the Devil, and he will flee from you' (James iv. 7).

'What time I am afraid, I will trust in Thee' (Psalm lvi. 3).

'I will trust, and not be afraid' (Isa. xii. 2)."

—*B. McCall Barbour.*

"I fear no foe, with Thee at hand to bless,
Ills have no weight, and tears no bitterness:
Where is death's sting? where, grave, thy victory?
I triumph still, if THOU abide with me."

PEACE—IN THE STORM

"Master, carest Thou not that we perish? And He arose, and rebuked the wind, and said unto the sea, Peace, be still. And the wind ceased, and there was a great calm."—Mark iv. 38, 39.

"WE see our Lord Jesus Christ doing that which is proverbially impossible. He speaks to the winds and they obey Him. He speaks to the waves, and they submit to His command. He turns the raging storm into a calm with a few words—'Peace, be still.' Those words were the words of Him Who first created all things. The elements knew the voice of their Master, and, like obedient servants, were quiet at once.

Let us lay this lesson up in our minds. With the Lord Jesus Christ nothing is impossible. No stormy passions are so strong but He can tame them. No temper is so rough and violent but He can change it. No conscience is so disquieted, but He can *speak peace* to it, and make it calm. No man ever need despair, if he will only bow down his pride, and come as a humble sinner to Christ. Christ can do miracles upon his heart.—No man ever need despair of reaching his journey's end, if he has once committed his soul to Christ's keeping. Christ will carry him through every danger. Christ will make him conqueror over every foe.—What though our relations oppose us? What though our neighbours laugh us to scorn? What though our place be hard? What though our temptations be great? It is all nothing, if Christ is on our side, and we are in the ship with Him. Greater is He that is for us, than all they that are against us."

—Rev. J. C. Ryle, D.D.

" Be still, my soul : thy God doth undertake
　To guide the future as He has the past.
Thy hope, thy confidence let nothing shake :
　All now mysterious shall be bright at last.
Be still, my soul : the waves and winds still know
　His Voice Who ruled them while He dwelt below."

FEAR NOT!

Trials should not be anticipated

"The cloudy and dark day."—Ezek. xxxiv. 12.

"WE are not to anticipate trial. God wants us to take the days as they come, building little fences of trust about each one, shutting out all that does not belong to it. We are not to stain to-day's blue sky with to-morrow's clouds. We are not to burden to-day's strength with to-morrow's loads. We are not to walk sadly in bright youth, when we have no sorrows, because we know that later in life we must meet pain and grief. 'Sufficient unto the day is the evil thereof.' Yet we should live in the glad days, so that when the sad days come they will not overwhelm us. For no matter how brightly the sun shines about us to-day, it will some time grow dark. No holy living, no kind of preparation beforehand, can keep the affliction away. That is not the way God blesses His children. Yet there are ways of living in the sunny days so that when the night comes we shall not be left in utter darkness.

One way is by storing our minds with the promises of God. . . . These promises, for which we had no use in the days of human joy, but which we took into our heart against the time of need, will now shine down upon us, and fill our gloom with sweet light from heaven. . . .

Another way is by keeping the vision clear all the time, between our souls and heaven. . . . Walk while ye have light, that the darkness overtake you not, swallow you not up. That is, in the days of earthly joy and prosperity, keep the view between your soul and heaven clear and open.

Still another way in which we may be prepared in the light for the darkness is suggested by our Lord Himself, in one of His teachings. 'While ye have the light, believe on the light, that ye may become sons of light.' But how can we get the light into our own life? Only by opening our heart to the love of Christ. . . . Be filled with Christ. This is the secret of comfort. Open your heart to His love, to His Spirit, to His peace, to His joy, to His life. Abide in Christ till Christ abides in you, until you are filled with all the fulness of God. Then *you need not fear any sorrow*, for the comfort is in yourself. . . . No darkness can make it dark in your soul, because the light of Christ shines there." —*Rev. J. R. Miller, D.D.*

"Trust God for to-morrow,
Though clouds may lower to-day
'Fear nots' are surely written
To drive despair away." (*H.M.G.*)

PEACE—AMIDST TROUBLE

" Let not your heart be troubled : ye believe in God, believe also in Me."—John xiv. 1, 27.

HOW unspeakably precious are the words of Jesus, as they tell us the secret of abiding rest, and unbroken peace, in the midst of all the distractions and confusions of this sin-scarred earth, now so full of sorrow and suffering. . . . Surely our Lord knew all that would befall His own, and almost baffle their faith, when He so lovingly and tenderly uttered the words which form the theme of the closing discourse of His life's ministry.

' Let not your heart be troubled,' are among the sweetest of all the gracious words that proceeded out of His mouth. They have lulled many a ransomed soul into the last sleep, as the tired body has sunk into the silence of death, and they have cheered the weary pilgrim along the valley, as they have told of the presence and the peace of Him Who giveth His beloved sleep. But we must not separate them from their context, lest we miss the meaning of their message. Our Lord at once points onward to the secret place of rest and comfort, as He tells of a faith that is fixed upon Him, Who is very God of very God, and Who claims the same confidence as that which has been reposed in the Father. ' Ye believe in God ; believe also in Me.' ' I and My Father are ONE.' It is upon this blessed ground we rest our all, as we seek to find that peace which the world can never give, and here we know that we have access into the Holiest, for He has said, ' I am the Way, the Truth and the Life, no man cometh unto the Father but by Me.' Thus emboldened, may we not enter into the rest that remains for the people of God, and claim that peace of God which passeth all understanding. . . . May we enter into our possessions, even as once more the Holy Spirit brings to our remembrance the things which He hath spoken. So shall we be saved from all anxious fears, and carking cares, and, however the floods may rise, and the waves lift up their voice, we shall know the secret of a life at rest in God ; and for us there will be the glad consciousness that no evil can befall us, neither shall any plague come nigh our dwelling."—*Rev. G. H. Lunn, M.A.*

FEAR NOT!

Satan—the source of fear

"God hath not given us the spirit of fear; but of power, and of love, and of a sound mind."—II Tim. i. 7.

"IT is clear that fear is not of God. God 'hath not given' it. From whence then does it come? It is only logical to infer that its source must be the Devil, and the infliction of it upon us is his design for our destruction. We would, therefore, affectionately say to all 'who are of a fearful heart'—courageously face the fact that the fear that enfeebles and unfits you is not of God, and that, being right with God, you should deliberately, by a definite act of will, refuse to take it from the Devil.

For the strengthening of such resolve and determination consider this further word of exhortation from the Lord. 'Submit yourselves therefore to God. Resist the Devil, and he will flee from you' (James iv. 7). As we comply with the conditions for deliverance from the Satanic power, the result shall be most surely experienced. Note carefully what these conditions for deliverance are, so that by no indifference or carelessness may we be deceived into the Devil's snares.

First, then, be sure that the life is whole-heartedly submitted to God; 'In all thy ways acknowledge Him' (Prov. iii. 5-6). 'Yield yourselves unto God' (Rom. vi. 13). Reckon on His presence within you; rely upon His wisdom to guide you, and His power to control and protect your entire being. Submission to God is the first essential condition for successful deliverance from the 'fears' of the Devil. When thus yielded to God, then 'Resist the Devil; and he will flee from you'. Thus saith the Lord! As, then, we are exhorted not to take fear from the Devil, let us be positive and practical in taking from God all the wealth of provision which He *has given* to us in Himself to meet our perpetual and ever-pressing need. Take, then, at this moment, what God *has* provided in Christ, and is offering to you dear reader, as full equipment for victory over all your 'fears'."
                                        —*B. McCall Barbour.*

'I take the promised Holy Ghost
I take the *power* of Pentecost
To fill me to the uttermost
    'I *take*'—'He undertakes.'

I simply take Him at His Word,
I praise Him that my prayer is heard,
And *claim* my answer from the Lord,
    'I *take*'—'He undertakes.' "

                                    (*Rev. A. B. Simpson, D.D.*)

PEACE—IN LIFE'S GETHSEMANE

"The peace of God which passeth all understanding."
—Phil. iv. 7.

"My peace I give unto you."—John xiv. 27.

"Father, if Thou be willing, remove this cup from Me : nevertheless not My will, but Thine, be done."—Luke xxii. 42.

"LORD arm me for the silence ! Often, in my hour of trial, I am brave when duty has to be done, and weak when it is over. In the first fire of the bereavement I have to rise up from among the dead. There are letters to be written ; there are sad offices to be performed ; there are friends to be bidden to the funeral. And I go through them calmly ; I feel as if something supported me ; men say, 'How bravely he bears it !' But, when the letters are finished, and the funeral is over, and the friends gone, then comes the misery, the despair. Save me, O Lord ! Save me from my own companionship ! Protect me from the solitude of my heart ; arm me against myself ! I have been strong in the hour of outward battle, because I heard the voices of human sympathy ; let me hear the voice of a greater sympathy, for the watch of the night ! I was able to withstand in the day, because there was work to be done ; help me in the shadows, when no man can work ! Teach me that the heart has a duty greater than the hand ! Teach me that I am not a perfect soldier when I can only fight ! Teach me that the courage which can endure is nobler than the courage that can strike ! Teach me the heroism of Gethsemane, when Thou hadst finished the work that was given Thee to do, and hadst only the weight that was given Thee to bear ! Thou hast girded me with the sword for the tumult ; clothe me with the breastplate for the silence ! My armour shall only be complete when I have done all and still shall stand."

—*Rev. George Matheson, D.D.*

"There is a peace that cometh after sorrow,—
    Of hope surrendered, not of hope fulfilled ;
A peace that looketh not upon the morrow,—
    But calmly on a tempest that is stilled.
A peace that lives not now in joy's excesses,—
    Nor in the happy life of love secure,—
But in the unerring strength the heart possesses
    Of conflicts won, while learning to endure.
A peace there is, in sacrifice secluded,—
    A life subdued,—from will and passion free
'Tis not the peace that over Eden brooded,
    But that which triumphed in Gethsemane."

(Anon.)

FEAR NOT!
The dark valley made bright

"Yea, though I walk through the valley of the shadow of death, I will fear no evil: for Thou art with me."—Psalm xxiii. 4.

"THIS unspeakably delightful verse has been sung on many a dying bed, and has helped to make the dark valley bright times out of mind. Every word in it has a wealth of meaning. 'Yea, though I *walk*,' as if the believer did not quicken his pace when he came to die, but still calmly *walked* with God. To walk indicates the steady advance of a soul which knows its road, and knows its end, resolves to follow the path, feels quite safe, and is therefore perfectly calm and composed. The dying saint is not in a flurry; he does not run as though he were alarmed, nor stand still as though he would go no further; he is not confounded nor ashamed, and therefore keeps to his old pace. Observe that it is not walking *in* the valley, but *through* the valley. We go through the dark tunnel of death and emerge into the light of immortality. We do not die, we do but go to sleep to wake in glory. Death is not the house but the porch; not the goal but the passage to it. . . . 'The *shadow* of death.' Nobody is afraid of a shadow, for a shadow cannot stop a man's pathway even for a moment. The shadow of a dog cannot bite; the shadow of a sword cannot kill; the shadow of death cannot destroy us. Let us not, therefore, be afraid. 'I will fear no evil.' He does not say there shall not be any evil; he has got beyond even that high assurance, and knew that Jesus had put all evil away; but 'I will *fear* no evil'; as if even his *fears*—those shadows of evil—were gone for ever. The worst evils are those which do not exist, except in our imagination. . . . We feel a thousand deaths in fearing one, but the Psalmist was cured of the disease of fearing. 'I will fear no evil'—not even the Evil One himself; I will not dread the last enemy; I will look upon him as a conquered foe, an enemy to be destroyed. 'For Thou art with me.' This is the joy of the Christian! 'Thou art with me.' "

—*Rev. C. H. Spurgeon.*

" ' I will fear no evil'! Rather will I dwell
  In happy muse on this—that I have THEE;
That surely Thou art with me—therefore all is well
  Great Wonder-worker Thou dost choose to be!
'I will fear no evil'! Nay—instead would know
  That 'unafraidness' which doth honour Thee
And say to each tormenting, fear-suggesting foe,
  That Christ hath gotten us the Victory."

(*J. Danson Smith.*)

PEACE—DEEPENED THROUGH TROUBLE

" The Lord's portion is His people."—Deuty. xxxii. 9.

" The Lord will bless His people with peace."—Psl. xxix. 11.

" SURELY such a promise should make the Church calm and hopeful under the most distressing circumstances, even though the earth be removed and the mountains be carried into the midst of the sea. It speaks little for our vital relationship to God when we are disturbed by every sound of tumult. Union with God should mean participation in the nature of God, not mere connection, but spiritual oneness ; not the union of a link, but the union of life. The good man may be violently tossed about, as if God had a controversy with him, yet in the depths of his heart there may be a great peace. The very stress, too, that is put upon him will give him a bolder and richer character if it be accepted filially, and deepen the peace which it threatened to destroy. The good man should not read the surface, or trouble himself with the accidents of the hour. The apostles, when cast down, were not destroyed ; when persecuted, were not forsaken. ' If God be for us who can be against us.' Let men who have no God, tremble and be dismayed when portentous shadows stretch over the earth, and reverberating storms shake the atmosphere, and lightning flashes like the sword of awakening vengeance ; but they who abide under the wings of the Almighty may,—

> ' The dark'ning universe defy
> To quench their immortality
> Or shake their trust in God.'

Two things are clear : out of God there is no peace : in God there is perfect peace. The good man meets every day with a hopeful spirit, and will meet his last day with the most hopeful spirit of all."

—*Rev. Joseph Parker, D.D.*

FEAR NOT!
Christd is nearer than circumstances

"Whoso hearkeneth unto Me shall dwell safely, and shall be quiet from fear of evil."—Prov. i. 33.

"**P**RESENT evil can be as much a nightmare as fear of the future. Many a soul, relieved from fear of future condemnation, is harassed by daily cares. There is the amazing hurry of modern life. There are the times when apprehension dreads impending woe, or mind and conscience seem entangled in the maze of some tortuous perplexity. There is opposition to our Christian efforts, or spurning of them by those who are unconcerned. Above all, there are the extraordinarily menacing clouds of the world-outlook.

Yes, circumstances throng. But Christ is nearer to us than circumstances. Opposition and contempt rage—but their fury is impotent to those who are bathed in the holy atmosphere of the peace of this promise—'shall dwell securely', free from care; 'shall be quiet from *fear* of evil'. All the foundations of the earth may seem to be out of course; dread judgment hangs ready to fall upon a reckless and rebellious world; but those who 'hearken' are 'secure', and may be 'quiet' even from 'fear'. The Master was unruffled in His busiest days: calm, and even joyful, in the prospect of His very suffering: will He not impart to His trusting servant His secret of peace—what He calls 'My peace', 'My joy'? We know He will. 'Let not your heart be troubled,' were His very words: 'ye believe in God, believe also in Me'.

But *to whom* is the promise given? It is to those who '*hearken*'. To these is the promise, and to these alone. And to hearken is more than to hear. It is a word betokening obedience—or, to put it even more fully, obedient trust, trustful obedience. Many *hear* repeatedly, but do not heed. Not even all who seem to *listen*, really 'hearken' in the sense just described.

For what do they heed who really hearken? A double call. There is that call 'Come unto Me', with its promise of 'rest' (Matt. xi. 28). But there is the accompanying call of the succeeding words—to 'take His yoke' and 'learn of Him'." —*The Christian.*

"In nothing be anxious: the Lord is at hand
In peace and in victory triumphantly stand:
Let nothing affright thee, and nothing dismay
For Jesus is coming! it may be to-day!"

(*M. E. Barber.*)

PEACE—ITS INCREASE

" The government shall be upon His shoulder . . . and
of the increase of His government and peace there shall be
no end."—Isa. ix. 6, 7.

" IS the government of your life upon His shoulder ?
It is well when the government of our lives rests
on the strong Son of God. . . . The moment of
definitely imposing the government upon the Lord Jesus
is generally a marked one in our lives. It stands out as
the first of a long series. It is the staple of a chain of
successive links, because we are always increasing that
government in proportion as we become more familiar
with our nature and opportunities, and as new depart-
ments of our life open up before us. . . . Just in proportion to the increase of His government will be the
increase of *your peace.* As the one extends so does the
other. And he who has extended the dominion of Jesus
to the furthest limits of his being will know most of the
peace that passeth understanding. There is Peace where
there is Unity ; where the soul has but one object to
engross its love and aim ; where it is able to count on the
illimitable stores of its King. . . .

What is your reply to the claim of Christ ? I urge
you to-day to humbly put the government of everything
that concerns your life upon the shoulders of Christ, and
then you will find that joy and peace will increase. Such
joy as thou hast never known ! Such peace as has never
before uttered its benison upon thy heart."

—*Rev. F. B. Meyer, D.D.*

" When Jesus, as Lord, I had crowned,
My heart with this peace did abound,
In HIM the rich blessing I found,
Sweet peace, the gift of God's love."
(*P. P. Bilhorn.*)

" Yield to the Lord, with simple heart,
All that thou hast and art !
Renounce all strength, but strength divine,
And *Peace* shall be forever thine ! "
(*Anon.*)

FEAR NOT!
Anxieties should be shared with God

"Be careful for nothing; but in everything by prayer and supplication with thanksgiving let your requests be made known unto God. And the peace of God, which passeth all understanding, shall keep your hearts and minds through Christ Jesus."—Philps. iv. 6-7.

"THE truth is that the way of peace and the path of deliverance from slavish anxiety can never be found through our own unaided resources. It is for this reason that the Apostle Paul, in writing to the Philippians, does more than urge his readers—'in nothing be anxious'—for he goes on to say: 'but in everything by prayer and supplication, with thanksgiving, let your requests be made known unto God'. It will be seen, therefore, that the first suggestion the Apostle makes is that we should share our anxieties with our Heavenly Father. He knows all about us: He remembers our frame: He knows that we are dust: and when we seek His face in the midst of all our difficulties, we have already made some progress along the path of peace. We have commenced the process of sharing our burden with Another.

It is not too much to say that the root trouble in every form of anxiety, so far as Christian people are concerned, is a definite want of faith. All forms of worry are the result of imperfect trust. . . . Here we see the wisdom of cultivating the spirit of faith even in our happiest hours, for, in the time of difficulty and need that same spirit of faith will come immediately to our rescue, and we shall find all our *consolation* in God, just as we found all our *happiness* in Him when the days were bright. . . . If we walk with the Lord day by day—whether skies be blue or overcast—we shall so cultivate and practice the Presence of God that when occasions of anxiety may arise, we shall be prepared, and in that same loving fellowship with Him we shall find complete deliverance. . . . Let us dare to trust Him, and, in that very act of simple trust, we shall find a deliverance from all our fears, and a relief from all our anxieties which can come in no other way."

—The Christian.

"Your Father knoweth all the crowding needs
That make a burden for the anxious heart;
And He Who every chirping sparrow feeds
Will not forget to play a Father's part:
Who doubts His love, a needless sorrow soweth,
Your Father knoweth."

—Rev. F. J. Exley, D.D.

PEACE—A GLORIOUS CERTAINTY

" Let him take hold of my strength, that he may make peace with Me ; and he shall make peace with Me."—Isa. xxvii. 5.

" ' MY strength ' ! Who is ' the strength of God ' ? Let Scripture answer :—' Let thy hand be upon the man of Thy right hand, upon the Son of man Whom Thou madest *strong*, for Thyself ' (Psl. lxxx. 17). ' Christ is the Power of God,'—the Daysman betwixt us, who has laid His hand upon us both (Job ix. 33). He, too, is ' our *peace*.' ' Being justified by faith we have peace with God.' ' Peace, not as the world giveth,' was His parting special legacy It is a sure and well-grounded peace, purchased by His atoning blood, and secured and perpetuated by His continual intercession. Hence the gracious Proposer of reconciliation adds the assurance—' And he shall make peace with Me.' It is a glorious certainty. Take hold of that arm, and salvation is sure. ' Believe on the Lord Jesus Christ and thou *shalt* be saved.' A present peace, a sure peace, a permanent peace ;—peace now, and peace for ever. ' None is able to pluck you out of His hand.'

' Awake, awake, put on strength, O arm of the Lord.' ' Give ear, O Shepherd of Israel, thou that leadest Joseph like a flock. . . . Stir up thy STRENGTH, and come and save us ' (Psl. lxxx. 1, 2). ' For I know the thoughts that I think toward you, saith the Lord, thoughts of peace, and not of evil, to give you an expected end ' (Jer. xxix 11)."—*Rev. J. R. Macduff, D.D.*

> " ' Thou wilt keep him in perfect peace,
>   Whose mind is stayed on Thee.'
> Is this Thy message, O Master ?
>   And is it meant for me ?
> Peace ? When all things are tending
>   To rob me of my peace ?
> When the storms of life are raging,
> Wilt Thou speak the word of peace ?
>   Thou wilt keep him in perfect peace
>   Whose mind is stayed on Thee.'
> Thou art my peace, in Thee alone
>   I find true peace to be.
> ' Great peace have they that love Thy law,'
>   Thy ' paths are paths of peace,'
> And when our minds are stayed on Thee
>   All fear and dread will cease."

Fairelie Thornton

FEAR NOT!

The blessedness of being still

"Be still, and know that I am God."—Psalm xlvi. 10.

"IN times of difficulty—be still! Thine enemies are plotting thine overthrow! They laugh at thy strong confidence! But hast thou not heard His voice saying: 'This is the way, walk ye in it'? Then leave Him to deal with thy foes, from whatever quarter they may come. He is thy Rock, and rocks do not shake. He is thy High Tower, and a high tower cannot be flooded. Thou needest mercy, and to Him belongeth mercy. Do not run hither and thither in panic! Just quietly wait, hushing thy soul, as He did the fears of His friends on the eve of Gethsemane and Calvary. 'Rest in the Lord, wait patiently for Him.' 'Be still, for He will not rest, until He hath finished the thing this day.'"

—Rev. F. B. Meyer, D.D.

"Have you taken it to Jesus—
  Have you left your burden there—
Does He tenderly support you—
  Have you rolled on Him your care?
O, the sweet unfailing refuge
  Of the Everlasting Arms:
In their loving clasp enfolded
  Nothing worries or alarms.

Have you taken it to Jesus—
  All the longings, hopes and fears:
All the many disappointments:
  All the sorrow, grief and tears?
Does He lovingly sustain you,
  Guard and guide, and cheer and bless?
Are you living in the sunshine
  Of His grace and righteousness?

Have you taken it to Jesus—
  Just the thing that's pressing now?
Are you trusting Him completely
  With the when, and where and how?
Oh, the joy of full surrender
  Of our life, our plans, our all:
Proving, far above our asking
  That God answers when we call.

Have you taken it to Jesus?
  'Tis the only place to go
If you want the burden lifted,
  And a solace for your woe:
Oh, the blessedness to nestle
  Like a child upon His breast
Finding ever, as He promised,
  Perfect comfort, peace and rest."

(Mrs. E. L. Hennessay.)

PEACE—THE CHRISTIAN MESSAGE

" Then the same day at evening, being the first day of the week, when the doors were shut where the disciples were assembled for fear of the Jews, came Jesus and stood in the midst, and saith unto them, Peace be unto you. . . . Then said Jesus to them again, Peace be unto you . . . as My Father hath sent Me, even so send I you."—John xx. 19-21.

" Preach the Gospel of Peace."—Rom. x. 15.

" HE spoke, we may be sure, with special reference to the state of mind of the eleven apostles, with special reference to the events of the last few days, and with special reference to their future ministry. ' Peace,' and not blame,—' peace,' and not fault-finding —' peace,' and not rebuke,—was the first word which this little company heard from their Master's lips after He left the tomb. It was meet, and right, and fitting, that it should be so, and in full harmony with things that had gone before. ' Peace on earth,' was the song of the heavenly host when Christ was born. Peace and rest of soul was the general subject that Christ continually preached for three years. Peace, and not riches, had been the great legacy which He left with the eleven the night before His crucifixion. Surely it was in full keeping with all the tenor of our Lord's dealings, that, when He revisited His little company of disciples after His resurrection, His first word should be ' Peace.' It was a word that would soothe and calm their minds.

Peace, we may safely conclude, was intended by our Lord to be the key-note to the Christian ministry. That same peace which was so continually on the lips of the Master, was to be the grand subject of the teaching of His disciples. Peace between God and man through the precious blood of atonement,—peace between man and man through the infusion of grace and love.—To spread such peace as this was to be the work of the Church. Any religion, like that of Mahomet, who made converts with the sword, is not from above but from beneath. Any form of Christianity which burns men at the stake, in order to promote its own success, carries about with it the stamp of an apostasy. That is the truest and best religion which does most to spread real, true peace."

—Rev. J. C. Ryle, D.D.

FEAR NOT!

A "Fear Not" for every day

"That we being delivered out of the hand of our enemies might serve Him without fear."—Luke i. 74.

"SOMEONE has counted 365 'fear nots' in the Bible. I suppose having found one for each day of the year he stopped counting. No wonder there is so much dread and terror in the world when the Bible is largely a neglected book. To the Israelites the message came: 'The Lord shall fight for you and ye shall hold your peace'. Solomon declared: 'Victory is of the Lord'. Zephaniah sang: 'The Lord thy God is in the midst of thee a Mighty One, He will save'. The Apostle Paul, out of a terrifying experience, wrote of his God: 'Who delivered . . . and doth deliver . . . and in Whom we trust that He will yet deliver'. Is there any need for fear with a God like that? Jesus said: 'Be not afraid, it is I'. The two phrases are interdependent. If we have Christ near, we need not be afraid.

We fear that many cannot gain peace because subconsciously there is disharmony deep in the soul. Just as the surgeon knows that it is useless to just cut the outer skin and draw blood, he must dig down as deep as the disease to eradicate the trouble; so in spiritual sickness the only way effectively to deal with the trouble is to be honest and ruthless with oneself, to face the worst with a fixed determination to settle the vexed question for ever. Reader, is your heart right with God? There is nothing to fear in this life, if the question of the next life is settled. Man has no cause for panic, if he possesses the peace of God. Let me say this on the authority of God's Word—You have broken God's law and transgressed His commands, but from His side there is no ground for continued hostility. He loves the sinner. Christ died to reconcile you to God. Read this—'Let the wicked forsake his way and the unrighteous man his thoughts and let him return unto the Lord, and He will have mercy upon him; and to our God for He will abundantly pardon'.

Why not make that 'abundant pardon' yours? With the full assurance of that pardon yours by faith, panic is impossible, peace is assured. Why not make certain of it now?"   —*Newman Watts* (*A London Journalist*).

"Child of My love, fear not the unknown morrow—
Dread not the new demand life makes on thee;
Thy ignorance doth hold no cause for sorrow,
Since what thou knowest not is known to Me."

(*Rev. F. J. Exley, D.D.*)

PEACE—EARTH'S ONLY HOPE

"For unto us a Child is born, unto us a Son is given : and the government shall be upon His shoulder : and His Name shall be called Wonderful, Counsellor, the Mighty God, The Everlasting Father, The Prince of Peace. Of the increase of His government and *peace* there shall be no end, upon the throne of David, and upon His kingdom, to order it, and to establish it with judgment and with justice from henceforth even for ever. The zeal of the Lord of Hosts will perform this."—Isa. ix. 6, 7.

"THE Only Hope for adjustment in the professing Church, for the restoration of the Jews to Palestine, and the settlement of disputes among the Nations of the Earth, is the Personal return of Christ. There will never be *peace and righteousness* until ' the King shall reign in righteousness ' (Isa. xxxii. 1).

Christ shall not fail, so let us look and long for Him. The late James Vaughan has expressed our true attitude as we look for the King to return : ' Oh, it is such a pleasant thing to watch. Pleasant to go up on the high door of prophecy, to turn the telescope of inspiration down the road where He will come. Pleasant in every trouble to feel in a moment He may come, and cut this trouble very short. Pleasant in every fear, however deep, to think that Christ's coming may be nearer than that which we fear. Pleasant to feel when the world knocks at your door that you can say I am keeping the place for Jesus ; and I cannot let you in. Pleasant in your work to hear conscience say, I think my dear Master would like to find me here. Pleasant, when all is happy, to double the happiness with the thought that He, too, will be soon here. And pleasant to wake up every morning and think, What can I do to-day to prepare the way for my Saviour. Pleasant to go to bed every night and feel His coming is one day nearer. Brethren, He is worth waiting for.' "—*Rev. F. E. Marsh, D.D.*

> " Jesus is coming ! sing the glad word !
> Coming for those He redeemed by His blood,
> Coming to reign as the glorified Lord !
>   Jesus is coming again !
>
> Jesus is coming ! His saints to release;
> Coming to give to the warring earth peace :
> Sinning, and sighing, and sorrow, shall cease ;
>   Jesus is coming again ! "

(El. Nathan.)

FEAR NOT!

Faith's value lies in its Object

"What time I am afraid."—Psalm lvi. 3.

"FEAR is a very real factor in life to-day. There is a definite sense of fear abroad, causing the stoutest hearts to apprehend the stealthy, irresistible approach of a peril they are unable to define. In personal life, too, fear raises its head. To be true to Christ and His Word is to encounter an increasing ostracism, if not unveiled contempt and hostility. Fears of temptation and evil are assailing, in unparalleled vehemence, the heart most set on righteousness.

The Bible, however, has anticipated our fears. Perhaps its most frequent exhortation is 'Fear Not'! And, as the things which it emphasizes are for emphasis in our own appropriation, we may have confidence that the fears in our hearts are but an anticipated peril of the pilgrim way, for which God has made complete and annihilating provision. . . . Thus, the cure for fear, in all its aspects, lies in our being able to say, 'What time I am afraid, I will trust in Thee'. This is the faith that overcomes fear. Now the value of our faith, lies not in itself, but in the OBJECT on which it is set. The faith that delivers from fear is set on Him Who gave His Son. 'Shall He not with Him also freely give us all things?' (Rom. viii. 32). This faith is *reasonable*. Where will you find a fuller provision, a more sure refuge? It is supported by all the promises of God. It is evidenced by the experience of all God's people.

> 'Did ever saint find this Friend forsake him?
> No not one, no not one!'

This faith that banishes fear is also *seasonable*—'What time I am afraid'—just when that fear grips you, in the stillness of the night, in life's sudden emergencies, or as you draw near to the revealings of eternity, that is the time to say: 'I will trust in Thee'. Then the soul's experience will be that of David in the last verse of this psalm (lvi): 'Thou hast delivered my soul from death; wilt Thou not deliver my feet from falling, that I may walk before Thee?'"

—Rev. W. Gist, M.A.

> "The raven He feedeth, then why should I fear?
> To the heart of the Father His children are dear
> So if the way darkens, or storms gather o'er,
> I'll simply look upward and trust Him the more."

(Selected.)

PEACE—AND PEACE-MAKING

" Blessed are the pure in heart : for they shall see God. Blessed are the *peacemakers* : for they shall be called the children of God."—Matt. v. 8, 9.

" AMONG the many arguments by which we may endeavour to stir ourselves and induce others to become *peacemakers*, probably the loftiest is the one which leads the Christian constantly to inquire, ' What is my Father doing ; what is my Father caring for ; in which direction are the energies of the Eternal Nature now proceeding. For, if I can only discover these, the truest policy for myself, for my blessedness, and the blessedness of others, is that I should concur with, and advance, so far as I can, these mighty movements.' Therefore the purity of heart in which a man sees God seems necessary, as the pre-requisite for the peacemaking which is occupying our thoughts. If day by day, before we started forth on our daily pilgrimage, we were only pure enough in heart to stand before the presence of the King, and to ascertain in which direction He was most strenuously occupied ; to learn from Him what great design He had in hand ; then, as sons of the Father and as brothers of Christ, we should become interested in that in which He was interested, and enthusiastic over that upon which He had set His heart. We should go forth day by day, saying, ' Whither are Thy steps leading, O Prince of Peace ? We, Thy young brothers and sisters, would fain place our foot-prints, where Thine have left their impress. There are homes that Thou art entering to allay fear, unrest and disquietude ; we will follow. Where there are hearts that are tossed like the restless sea, over which Thou art about to speak Thy ' peace be still,' we will breathe it also. And where healing, rest-giving ministries have to be performed to men, then we will be there, too, to further Thee in Thy work.' There is not much hope of any of us, with our limited resources and powers, accomplishing much of this work of *peacemaking* in the world if we look only to ourselves. But our power is immensely multiplied when we have learnt to see God ; to live in communion with Christ ; to open our being to the blessed Holy Spirit, the Dove of Peace, that we may co-operate with God, and, watching Him, may do in earth what He is doing in heaven. ' Blessed are the pure in heart : for they shall see God.' ' Blessed are the peace-makers ; for they shall be called sons of God.' See how the two are associated."—*Rev. F. B. Meyer, D.D.*

FEAR NOT!

Fear has always a way of escape

"Why are ye troubled? And why do thoughts arise in our hearts."—Luke xxiv. 38.

LET us admit, quite frankly, that many of us are forfeiting the joy of life, and the joy of Christ's salvation, through our morbid fears of the future. The tragedy is that all our fears should be connected with to-morrow. We have no fear of to-day. We have work to do, and bread to eat, and friends to love, and, for the most part, a fair measure of health and strength. The trouble is never with to-day: it is always with to-morrow. As a general rule, fear is not concerned with what has happened, but with what may happen. . . . When we consider this fact in all its bearings, we can see how lovingly Jesus dealt with men. 'O men,' He cried, 'how little you trust God. Do not be afraid of to-morrow, for to-morrow can take care of itself.'

Possibly most of us would agree, as we look back over the pathway of life, that we have found that the circumstances and events of life are never so bad as they appeared to the eye of a fearful anticipation. With every trial God provides a way of escape; not, necessarily, the way we should have chosen, but a way in which we can walk if we have the mind. No event of life, when we overtake it and come up to it, is quite as bad as we had feared.

> 'Ye fearful saints! Fresh courage take
> The clouds ye so much dread
> Are big with mercy, and shall break
> With blessing on your head.'

There are few things that can more swiftly rob life of its joy and peace than morbid fears. Perfect love casteth out fear, and God is Love; which means that only God, by His Holy Spirit, can cast out the evil thing. To be free from fear, and free from bondage, is to be the blessed of the Lord. Have we not proved our Saviour's power to help us in days that are past? Then why should we be in a state of paralysis regarding the future? Can we not trust Him ever where it is impossible to trace Him? Such a mood, such a spirit of faith, will make us triumphant all along the line; and instead of wearing ourselves out by torturing fears about to-morrow, we shall be flinging all our strength into the tasks that call us to-day."

—*"The Life of Faith"*.

"Peace, perfect peace; the future all unknown?
Jesus we know, and He is on the Throne!"

PEACE—ITS REIGNING BEAUTY

" **Let the peace of God rule in your hearts.**"—**Col. iii. 15.**

" **S**T. PAUL exhorts us to let peace rule in our hearts. A marginal reading suggests another rendering— ' Let the peace of Christ arbitrate in your hearts.' It is to sit on the throne and have undisputed sway in the life. When, in the circumstances of any day, things arise which naturally trouble us, and would break into the calm and composure of our hearts, peace is to sit as arbiter, settling all conflicts of feeling, and bringing all strifes and differences to quiet adjustment. We are exhorted to let this peace rule. So, we can hinder its ruling if we will. It cannot rule unless we let it. . . . We need to look well, therefore, to the matter of the growth of loving peace in our life. Wherever it rules in the heart, it produces beauty in the disposition. It makes the whole life more and more loving. . . . The trouble with us is that we do not let this peace rule in us. Instead, we let a thousand other things—cares, disappointments, discontents, anxieties, fears, doubts, rule and mutiny against the rightful, heart-ruler. No wonder we have so little of the reign of quietness and calmness in us. If we would let peace take its place on the throne, and control all our life, it would soon grow into beauty. Then joy would sing its sweet songs wherever we go. We do not begin to realize the blessings that a heart, truly controlled by the peace of God, will bring into our life. We do not know the possibilities of loveliness of character there are in us, if only we would let peace dominate everything. We do not dream of the good we might do in the world, the comfort we might be to others, and the cheer and inspiration we might give to discouraged ones, those who are hard beset, and those who are in sorrow, if we would let the peace of Christ arbitrate in our hearts. We do not know how many souls we might win for Christ, how many lives we might redeem from low things and evil ways, if only the peace of Christ dwelt in us, transforming us into the beauty of the Lord. Nothing so wins others to better things as the influence of a sweet, disciplined and radiant personality."—*Rev. J. R. Miller, D.D.*